THE I

Confe..... .... j

MW00906012

More about *Discovering the Bright Warrior*:

"Here is a story that both informs and transforms the reader. Writing from personal insight and front-line experience, Joan Johannson brings us face to face with the dehumanizing treatment of the unemployed, forces us to confront our own stereotypes about poverty, and shakes us out of the inaction that comes from either complacency or despair. While this book is a scathing indictment of Canada's blame-the-victim approach, it is also an inspiring story of one individual's struggle to transform fear and anger into political action and positive change. It is testimony to the strength of the human spirit and the good that comes from collective action."

JUDY WASYLYCIA-LEIS
MP for Winnipeg North Centre

"A passionate description by a Metis woman of courage and compassion on a spiritual journey. The warrior spirit described in constructive and contemporary terms."

WAYNE HELGASON
Executive Director, Social Planning Council of Winnipeg

"The journey that Joan describes, from negative anger to hopeful warrior, has something to say to all who struggle for social justice in a hostile world."

BILL BLAIKIE
MP for Winnipeg Transcona

Discovering
THE BRIGHT

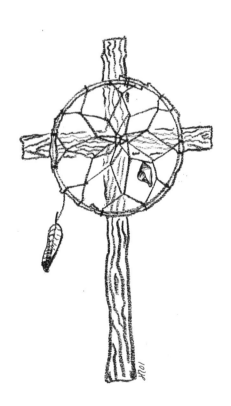

AN AUTOBIOGRAPHY BY
Joan Johannson

WARRIOR

Confessions
of a
Social Activist

For Lawrence

God bless you

Joan

Berserkr Press
Winnipeg, Manitoba, Canada

FIRST PUBLISHED IN 2001 BY
Berserkr Press
Winnipeg, Manitoba, Canada

© **Joan Johannson**
for information about permission to
reproduce selections from this book write to:
Berserkr Press, 277 Lipton Street, Winnipeg,
Manitoba, Canada, R3G 2H2
We encourage these ideas to be widely shared and discussed.
PLEASE FEEL FREE TO DIRECT QUESTIONS TO:
brightwarrior@mts.net

TYPESET AND DESIGN BY
Ampersand Compass Associates
COVER DESIGN BY
Gary Styrchak
CROSS AND DREAMCATCHER ILLUSTRATION BY
Holly Nelson

Printed and bound in Canada
First published in 2001

National Library of Canada Cataloguing in Publication Data
Johannson, Joan, 1943-
  Discovering the bright warrior
  Includes bibliographical references and index.
  ISBN 1-896474-05-5
1. Johannson, Joan, 1943-
2. Poverty—Canada.
3. Distributive justice—Canada.
4. Social reformers—Canada—
Biography. I. Title.
HC120.P6J58 2001   362.5'092   C2001-910821-4

DEDICATION

To Robert

For thirty-five years we have shared a life.
His thoughts and mine are so intertwined that
who knows which thoughts belong to who.

ACKNOWLEDGEMENTS

I became a social activist because in the 1960s I attended the University of Winnipeg and joined the Student Christian Movement. The Student Christian Movement opened my eyes to the Christian gospel as both a message of hope to a suffering and broken world, and a call to justice.

Over the years I have been involved in numerous social issues. But it was only when I became unemployed and entered the world of poverty that I really learned what it meant to struggle for justice. For seven years I was the Chairperson of the Canadian Association of the Non-Employed. I want to thank the people of CANE. They have taught me so much about life and the courage to survive.

In the daily struggle to survive I came close to despair. But Robert and I found St. Margaret's Anglican Church. The people of St. Margaret's have supported us in so many ways. I thank them for their encouragement, financial contributions, and most of all their prayers.

Finally, I want to thank my loving family, husband Robert and children Elizabeth, Catharine, and Michael. Knowing that I am loved and cherished is the greatest gift of all. Thank you especially to Catharine and Robert who edited and published this book. They believed in the "Bright Warrior" and they saw it through to print. I am indeed blessed.

DISCOVERING THE BRIGHT WARRIOR
Confessions of a Social Activist

Table of Contents

PREFACE

We are forcing our sons and daughters to be slaves.
CANADIAN COUNCIL OF CHURCHES,
HALIFAX G7, JUNE 1995

We have to stop being slaves, and we have to start thinking
for ourselves; we have to start standing up and resisting.
JOAN NEWMAN KUYEK,
CANADIAN DIMENSION, MAY/JUNE 1998

IT TOOK ME FIVE YEARS to discover the Bright Warrior. When I began this book the working title was *Sleepwalking to Slavery*. The image of slavery began with a discussion I had with my daughter Catharine. She had come home from India where she had been on a Leadership Development course for the World Student Christian Federation. She said "Mom, I met the first freed bonded labourer and here is his picture." His name is Maya Thar Darika. In India the landowners lend workers money and charge interest. But wages are so low, and the interest so high that the workers have no hope of ever paying the money back. When they die their children are responsible for the debt. Finally the people in the community organized and took action to end debt slavery. By 1994, 6000 bonded labourers had been freed.

I began to think about all the university students like my children that were amassing high debts. I thought about the people I knew in CANE who had university degrees and student loans and who were on welfare and trying to pay these loans off. I thought about the people who phone them and harass them and threaten them. These debt slaves are my friends and my children. Then, of course, there is workfare and wage slavery. We also read in the Globe and Mail that waiters are serving in restaurants in Ontario as "volunteers," but they get to keep the tips. The manager of one of these restaurants is quoted as saying "Our system is beautiful . . . They are not slaves." Whether someone is working for tips or is on welfare, the despair and the destitution, the powerlessness is slavery.

As the years went by I kept thinking and writing about slavery and freedom. I also kept wondering why people seemed indifferent to what was happening to their fellow citizens. I gradually decided that the problem is not so much indifference as lack of information, and thus lack of understanding. Most Canadians do not know what is happening to their fellow citizens. We think we see what is happening to us, to Canada. But we only see bits and pieces of the puzzle because we are only given bits and pieces by the main-stream media. We have been put to sleep by a series of hypnotic mantras such as "There are jobs out there if you really look for them." The mantras change. We used to be lulled into believing that there is no alternative by the mantra "The deficit is our number one problem." Now that most governments have balanced their books, we are told that high taxes are the problem. The continual thirty second sound bite solutions, and lack of thoughtful discussion of alternatives, has put most citizens to sleep. So my book became *Sleepwalking to Slavery*.

People are interested in the stories of other people. However, the story of the struggles and despair of individual Canadians is seldom told. Rather, the story of what is happening is being told through statistics, through bureaucrats and politicians. Canadians who are not directly affected by unemployment and poverty look at the television news and are told the latest unemployment statistics. I remembered that Stalin said "One death is a tragedy; a million deaths is a statistic." One death is a tragedy because that one death is of a living breathing person who has a story, and it could be my story. I decided to tell the stories of the people of CANE, of the people I have met who struggle for justice and of the people I have met who close their eyes and walk away.

I know that stories are more than what has happened. I learned this from the media. Whenever I spoke with a person from the media he or she would ask "How do you feel about that?" They assume that people want to know the answer to this question. People want to know how the non-employed (unemployed, part-time, minimum wage, contract workers) feel about their situation. It is impossible to answer that question in a thirty second sound bite. So I had to write a book, in the hope that I could do justice to the question and to the answer.

Section I explores the negative feelings people experience. Underlying all negative feelings is that incredible force of fear. Chapter One begins with a discussion of fear. The other negative feelings follow. We live in a society where the first question is always "Who is to blame?" Chapter Two looks at feelings of guilt, blame and shame. Then Chapter Three looks at despair, caused by the feeling of powerlessness. Finally, there is the negative feeling that continually trapped me. Chapter Four considers anger. All four feelings were so powerful in my life that it is painful even now to go back over them. Even though I no longer experience life in that emotional context, I know it so well. Life in the negative circle still has power over people, and I do not want to forget the power, or the fact that so many live there.

After the individual stories are told, the story of our country can be explored. Each person grows up and lives in a family, a neighbourhood, a city, town or rural area and in a nation. We are not individual atoms. Our lives are lived in context, in a specific time and place. There are four factors that determine how we live out our lives in the time and place we inhabit. Section II discusses those four variables. First, Chapter Five is about how we view reality, specifically economic reality. Our reality is determined by our perceptions. When we listen to politicians, they view Canada, its problems and solutions through their particular lens. And each party is absolutely sure that their analysis is reality. Chapter Six is about how our values shape everything we see and do. For most people their values are unconscious, learned as a child and seldom examined. Values are usually not part of the ongoing debates about the country and its people. Chapter Seven is about how we make decisions based on all those perceptions and values. The media is one of the most critical factors in shaping those decisions. Finally, we act. The society reacts to poverty in specific ways. There are usually two responses - charity or justice. Chapter Eight explores what these words mean.

After I had written Section I and Section II, the really tough part began. I had to discover "how to" move into the alternative emotional space of peace. Bit by bit, I dug into my experiences and knowledge. I searched out books and material in the library. I soon realized that there is practically nothing available to help people who are struggling for justice and who feel overwhelmed by negative emotions.

Gradually, I worked my way through Section III. Chapter Nine shows how to move from fear to faith. Chapter Ten explores forgiveness and reconciliation. Chapter Eleven shows that hope is possible. As I finished each chapter I felt better and better. But it was not until I reached Chapter Twelve that the final and most important shift took place. It was during the researching and thinking about anger that the Bright Warrior emerged. It took me five years to transform my life as a social activist. Each of us have a story to share. I was recently reminded of the power of story. My husband Robert, my friend Michael, and I were whizzing down Portage Avenue in my son's little red sports car. We were returning from an evening with university students from across Canada. We had once been young and at university together, and the evening had brought back old memories. We had been in the Student Christian Movement in the 1960s. Now we sat in a circle with students from the 1990s. Stan McKay, an Aboriginal church leader, was leading the discussion. Stan had a dream catcher. He began by saying his name, and what his name meant to him. Then he passed the dream catcher around the circle. Each one of us shared our names and what our names meant to us. After his talk we again passed the dream catcher. This time we reflected on what we had heard Stan say, how his story touched us, and we shared a part of our story.

I now could say that my name was Bright Warrior. I could share a little of my story with the students of today who care about justice. My hope is that everyone is able to find a circle where the dream catcher is passed around, and where they can tell their story.

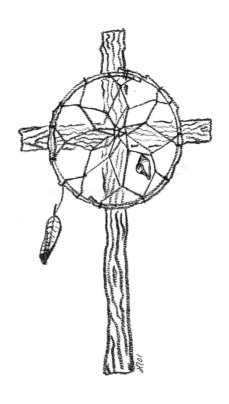

SECTION I
How Do You
Feel About That?

We are the people, listen to us.
CANE CONFERENCE, DECEMBER 10, 1994

H OW DO YOU FEEL ABOUT THAT? The reporters always ask me "How do you feel about that?" I can't begin to tell them in 30 seconds. But it's all the time I am given. It's not enough. I have to write a book.

When the reporters ask us how we feel, they are asking a question like the one Phil Donahue used to ask on his talk show. Only he would feed you the expected answer. He would say "Doesn't it make you mad?" Most reporters do not have to say that. It is inherent in the question. They assume that the answer is "It makes me so mad; it makes me so sad; so guilty; so depressed." How surprised they would be if I said "I feel a peaceful strength that enables me to go on."

We are expected to have all the negative feelings. In our society when bad things happen to us, we are expected to say "That makes me so depressed" or "He made me furious." Those outside people or forces did bad things to me, and I feel bad. And it is true that we do feel bad. We feel terrible.

For several years a few people from CANE attended an annual retreat for the unemployed given by St. Benedict's Retreat and Conference Centre. The first year we went there were twenty-seven people, and nine were from CANE. We had come to have a good time- free food, meeting new people, hopefully learning new things. The other eighteen people were there because they were recently unemployed, or their spouses were unemployed. The feelings that came from those people hit me like a shock wave. The anger and fear and guilt and despair were overwhelming. It was probably the first time that these people had the opportunity to talk about what had happened to them. I doubt if they would have told a reporter about their pain, but they were able to share their feelings with each other. It was a safe place to cry.

It is natural to feel bad when you lose your job. It is a shock; it is a death. In our society it is a death of one's identity. We are all so caught up in our job, what we do to make money, when the job goes we are knocked off our feet. I talked to a friend the other day. She and her husband are very knowledgeable about what is happening in our society, but he worked for the CBC and was recently laid off. She said "I can't believe how hard he is taking it. I keep saying it's not about you personally. But he feels it personally."

We know how badly people feel and some organizations try to help the newly laid off. The nurses' union set up a workshop for laid off health care workers. It was an opportunity to deal with the shock of being laid off. It was an opportunity to deal with fear, anger, depression and guilt. Although the workshops were widely advertised, very few people attended. The Canadian Mental Health Association also ran workshops for people newly laid off and these also were not well attended. My guess is that people who lose their jobs still feel that somehow it is their fault and they are ashamed and unable to reach out to the resources available.

Whether or not someone attends a workshop, after a while the initial feeling of shock wears off. Then the question "How do you feel?" relates to the job search. Here is where it gets interesting. The society conspires to do two opposing things at once. The job-finding club attempts to make you feel good. It pumps you up! On the other hand, the income support systems attempt to make you feel bad. One system gives you half the income you had before. The other system forces you to use up all of your money before you can receive help. In Winnipeg, you cannot have more than $10 dollars left in your pocket. Then you are forced to live not in poverty, but in destitution. I have a letter from the City of Winnipeg that states the welfare program is a program of destitution.

The intentional manipulation of people's lives, their resources and their feelings is done with the best of intentions by the powers that be. Countless harm has been done to people by the psychological theory of Behaviourism which has spread like a gray cloud over all our lives.

The carrot and the stick theory of human behaviour, as understood by the average lay person, states that you can motivate people to do what you want them to do. In this case what everyone wants the non-employed to do is to go out and get a well-paying job with a secure future. The motivation comes through a series of well-directed carrots and sticks, called "incentives" and "disincentives" by an unending line of politicians.

When Lloyd Axworthy was still the Minister of Human Resources Development, I used to listen to him expounding this theory. One weekend I heard him state on *Sunday Morning Live* that the Unemployment Insurance system was a "disincentive to work." The same weekend, on CBC Radio's *The House*, I heard him state that changes to Unemployment Insurance would provide a stronger "incentive to work." This is a familiar refrain. Don McGillivary reminded us "Support programs now in place must be re-focused to provide the unemployed with incentives."[1]

The changes in our social safety net, including the recent Child Benefit changes, all have this underlying theme and they are supported by federal and provincial governments of all political stripes. Whether it is Glen Clark in BC, or Bonnie Mitchelson in Manitoba, the rationale is to give working people the Child Tax Credit and to claw it back from people on welfare. The theory goes that this will give the people on welfare an incentive to find work.

The effect of taking money away from the poorest members of our society is that people feel bad. The assumption is that if you make people feel bad, by taking away the little they have, they will be motivated to get out there and get a job. The issue of whether there are enough jobs for everyone is not considered. Here is the great flaw in the carrot and stick theory. When people feel attacked, hit with a stick if you will, the usual human response is fight or flight. I don't usually see the fight response. The people who strike out in violence towards themselves or others usually end up in the justice system, or the mental health system. I usually have contact with the people who despair. After the last round of welfare cuts in Manitoba, on May 1, 1996, I noticed a drop in attendance at CANE meetings. When I would phone and talk to people I found many were feeling so depressed they could not get up the energy to come to meetings.

At the same time that people are feeling worse and worse from having no job and no money, they are herded into job-finding clubs. I have talked to countless non-employed people who have gone to every kind of job-finding club, both private and public. In all cases the major strategy is "Pump them up!" After three weeks people come out feeling positive and ready to tackle the job search once again. Unfortunately, if they do not get a job this time the valley of despair that soon appears is deeper than ever. The ups and downs of the emotional roller-coaster are greater on each successive ride.

It is not necessary to stay on the roller coaster. There are ways to survive the despair, and to be emotionally healthy in the midst of a cruel and uncaring society. But before we look at the possibilities of hope and courage, of faith and forgiveness, it is important to look at, and to understand, the suffering of the people.

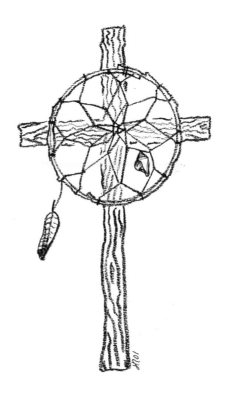

CHAPTER 1
WILL THERE BE CAMPS?

*When you are living on S.A. (social assistance) you're always
terrified. One little slip and they say good-bye . . . It's like
walking on egg shells. You're always so careful.*
CANE MEMBER

It's not a nice way to live, fearing your fellow citizens.
FRANCIS RUSSELL, WINNIPEG FREE PRESS, APRIL 25,1995

LAST NIGHT THE FEAR CAME AGAIN. I got up and went downstairs. There is no point in laying in bed. You know you won't go back to sleep. How many hours will you be up watching the early morning programs, the re-runs, the talk shows? There is no use crying, the tears have been and gone long ago. All that's left is the fear, a body that is rigid and a mind that seeks diversion.

A lowly foot soldier, in the losing side of an unending war, is often afraid. There is no end in sight. Day after day is spent pushing back the fear, but at night the unconscious wins. Keeping up a brave front, sometimes by turning the fear into anger, only lasts so long. At night, that's when the fear comes and stays. All my fellow companions on this lonely road. How many of you are up this night? How many tears are shed in the darkness? All the people, men and women and their children, in the dark hours afraid of what another day brings.

This room where I sit and watch television at three in

the morning has all my precious things: the pictures of the children, the books I love. It is a space that I have created. It is my home. How many have lost their homes? Sally[2] used to live in a three bedroom house in the suburbs. Now she lives in one room in a boarding house. Mike used to live in a one bedroom apartment. Now he lives in one room. Linda and Ruth, well-educated adults, used to live in apartments. Now they live with their parents. Will I too lose my home? I'll walk instead of taking the bus. I'll eat less. Please God, don't let me lose my home.

Money goes first to house payments and utilities. One day there is nothing left. I will go to the food bank. I too can swallow my pride. I phone the number and am told where to go. I walk down to the church. There, giving out the food, is an old friend. He and I have spent many hours fighting for justice for many people. But now I live in a different world: the world of fear and of poverty. I smile and say hello and take the food. I never go back.

Others never go. They count each nickel three times and they make bread. One mother at the 1994 CANE Conference shared her story and her fear.

> *"Do I buy milk or meat? Have we enough lentils and beans or peanut butter to give protein this week? What about fresh vegetables, fruit, rice? I have got ingredients to make bread, so that's okay. What if we do not pay all the heating bills again? Maybe we can take $10 from that for food."*

Others, many others of my friends, go to the food banks now. Of course, what you get is so little that it doesn't chase the fear away. The other day my friend Sally was at my house. We were going to a meeting and it was supper time. I wasn't sure if they were going to feed us there. I said to Sally "Here, take an apple. We'll have an apple before we go." She would not take it at first. She was afraid that if she took it, one of my children would not have an apple. I told her that it was okay. She does not get enough to eat. But she cares about the children. Oh my friend! Will your fear be lessened one day? Will you and your children have enough to eat?

It's funny. Nobody believes that people are starving. People living in destitution are hidden in rooms somewhere. Occasionally there is a story about homeless people, but I don't think I have ever seen a story about hungry people. After all, there are food banks aren't there? I knew people in Canada were hungry fifteen years ago. I was working for a research project called Neighbourhood Parenting Support Project. I went through the West Broadway area of Winnipeg interviewing parents. Many of them didn't eat for the last few days of the month. They had to make sure their children ate.

The parents didn't complain then and they don't complain now. For if you complain the powers that be might take away what little you have. The fear of the system is the greater fear. The fear is too powerful. We seldom share it with each other. To bring it out in the daylight might finally destroy the fragile place of normalcy that each of us have built.

The other day Steve brought a letter he had received from the welfare office. They apparently had overpaid him for a utility bill somewhere along the way. The letter announced that there would be fifty dollars deducted from his cheque next month. We heard him say it. My heart stopped. There was silence. We knew there had been a Welfare Action Line staffed by volunteers to help people in cases like this, but it had closed down last year. They were getting fifty calls a morning, and they just could not keep up. Had our fear finally made us all cowards, or had too many of us fought for too long?

Not only have we lost too often, the rules keep getting worse and worse. In May 1996, the rules were again changed in Manitoba. The Conservative government announced that all "employable" people on welfare, which now included mothers with children over six years old, would now have to seriously job search. We were told that mothers with children under six years would not be affected.

Mary, who lives with her daughter and grandson, came to a meeting. She told us that now mothers with children under six were being forced to job search. But more significantly, they were expected to sign a form, a contract. This contract said that if they did not carry out their job search as laid out for them, they would lose fifty dollars a month or be completely cut off welfare. We knew that "single employables" were expected to sign contracts. Some of our group had been pressured to do so. They had not, and in some cases had caused a minor rebellion in the job-finding clubs they were in. We knew that legally no one could be forced to sign the form. But they were signing it. When the person who decides whether you get your cheque this month says "Sign this" you sign.

Five years later there is an NDP government in Manitoba. But people are still being forced to sign the contract. People are losing fifty dollars a month, and in some cases losing one hundred dollars a month. There is still no organization to help people appeal such draconian measures. Thankfully, there are a few people around who volunteer advice to those who have lost their rightful money unfairly. Each time I hear the details of another case my heart breaks.

How fearful it is to be caught in large bureaucratic institutions. People who do not know you, or care about you, make life and death decisions about your life. In Manitoba you can be cut off welfare if you do not "satisfy the Director of Welfare." I have this vision of Jabba the Hutt, the monster who must be satisfied.

Laughter is a good way to chase the fear away. When we had our 1994 CANE Conference, there were so many talented people there. We made up a skit about Lloyd Axworthy applying for welfare. We howled with laughter. When he was told by one worker that he was not qualified for anything that was available, we laughed. When we saw him ordered out of the office of another worker for bringing in a cup of coffee, we laughed. Some knew this had really happened to one of us, but it is good to laugh in the midst of pain and fear.

Those who have to cope with the existing welfare system know very well the worker who orders you out of his or her office. If your welfare worker has had a bad day and you do not treat him as he expects, then "come back next week." If you are frustrated because you have no money for food, or rent, or utilities and you raise your voice in the welfare office, then "come back next week." If you have not made enough of an effort to job search this month, then your cheque this month is reduced by fifty dollars. There are also people in the system who bend over backwards to help. Kevin got a job last month because his employment counsellor told him about a job for which he would be perfect. John's worker gave him a bus pass last month.

The problem is that you never know. You never know if you will be treated with dignity, or as one of those "lazy welfare bums." Everyone is treated differently. Not everyone is asked to sign the contract that means that you lose fifty dollars next month if you do not satisfy the Director of Welfare's representative. I know that there are rules and regulations in a policy book somewhere, but the people from CANE have not yet been able to get our hands on one. It is an ongoing struggle to get information. Decisions are made about people's lives and we do not even know why, or what the rules are.

Fear comes also from confusion and uncertainty. It is not only the people who live their lives wondering when the next blow from the welfare office will fall. All those searching for work, day after day, week after week, month after month live in a world of confusion. People are told to get a good resume, learn interview skills, network, and then you will get a job. In the real world you seldom get a response to your application. When I was actively job searching I only applied for jobs for which I was qualified. Five years ago I used to get interviews. Now I do not even get a "Thank you for your application." I often listen to people describe their job search. There is a real sense of confusion. They will say "I did what I was supposed to do." "Why didn't I get an interview?" "What more am I supposed to do?" What we are told will happen and what actually happens is radically different. This kind of discrepancy can literally drive people crazy.

It is not only the people who are job-searching and who are struggling to get through another day who live in a confusing world. We are all confused and fearful about the changing world we live in. The changes that are now happening are as great as the changes of the Industrial Revolution. No one ever expects such radical change. In Canada, especially with the social security system that we had built in the 1960s and 1970s, we thought nothing too terrible could happen to us.

One of the greatest and most horrifying changes for me, and for many, is constantly being approached by people begging for money. Our friend Susan once said that she always wanted to go to India, but she had been afraid that she would not be able to handle dealing with all the beggars. She does not have this problem any more. She has become adapt at handling the beggars on the street. Each one of us has developed our own particular response. To my horror the other day I had someone come to the door asking for help. I guess that is next.

When did this brave new world begin? Although the ground work was laid twenty-five years ago, most of us began to take notice when the first Free Trade debate began. I remember going to a public meting in the Walker Theatre in Winnipeg. It was one of the many events focussing on the Free Trade agreement. The speaker was Maude Barlow of the Council of Canadians. She spoke eloquently about what was happening and what was likely to happen if the Free Trade agreement was implemented. One of the issues was what would happen to our social security system. The prediction was that it would gradually be eroded. In the question period a man got up and said he was very afraid of what would happen. Then he asked, in a puzzled and confused voice "But why would they do that to us?"

I think of that question now, years later, and I marvel. He was confused and unhappy and fearful of the future. But he said "Why would they do that to us?" He did not say "Why would they do that to me?" We used to think of a very broad and all-encompassing "us" in Canada. There was diversity in income and background, but the ordinary Canadians were in this together.

Now we are more and more divided into "us" and "them." We are so confused we do not even know who is "us" and who is "them." Those at the bottom with nothing are taught to blame each other. The other day someone new wandered into a CANE meeting. We were just finishing up. I started to explain who we were and what we were doing. He immediately started to say that the government should get tough on those drunks on welfare. It turns out, of course, that he is on welfare. I say to him that most of the people at the meeting are on welfare. Surely we need to think about what we need to live on, rather than a crack down on the few who abuse the system. (All studies show it is 3 to 5% who abuse the system.) Let's work on creating a decent income support system for all of us. I do not think that I got through to him. I have had this discussion numerous times over the years. The isolated individual who lives in fear often reacts by searching for someone to blame and he picks the group that the mainstream media blames. The "them" he blames are the mythical "welfare bums." He does not see that he is also considered one.

The people who work in the welfare system certainly fear the people they are supposed to serve. There are now glass windows, probably bulletproof, separating the "clients" and workers. As the violence in the society rises, so does the fear and so do the walls. There is not only bulletproof glass at the welfare office. There are more and more apartments with locked doors and security systems. And there are guard dogs. The fear is in every community, not just the places where the rich live. The core area is also a place of fear. A headline reads "Living scared in the no-zone."[3] The no-zone refers to the core area, where people are no longer able to get house insurance. The article refers to the big dogs, the condemned houses and the writer says "It looks like a civilization in decline."

For the rich, there is a way to escape this civilization in decline. Francis Russell states, "Rich take to the barricades."[4] She talks about the walled cities. Just north of Toronto, near Aurora, Ontario is one of Canada's new walled cities. On the top of those walls, apparently there is barbed wire. At the gates there are security guards. Michael Valpy picks up the theme of the walled cities. In "Walling out the World"[5] he muses on what a lady in the Kelowna walled city or gated community says. She says "you never see a stranger here." His response is "You don't know whether the number of street beggars is increasing, if they are not allowed to beg on your streets." At first I thought "How could you not know?" Then I remembered my aunt and uncle who live in a walled city in Cranbrook, BC. They told me how convenient it is. There are stores of all kinds inside the walls so you never have to leave.

The walls, of course, are an outward symptom of a society that is more and more divided. For years the vast majority of Canadians, no matter their income, thought of themselves as "middle class." We thought of ourselves as a classless society. Today Canadian society is fracturing along class lines. When Valpy writes about these issues he is appalled at what we are becoming. Others talk about the literal walling off of civil life[6]. In William Thorsell's reflections on the matter he sees those behind the walls as walled off, and protected from the pathologies of the underclass. He is talking about me and my friends, the one-fifth of Canadians who live in poverty.

There is another way to protect the well-off from "us." Those who are a threat, perceived or real, can be put behind walls, walled in. Prisons and work camps are set up for those who are angry and hopeless, and who lash out at society and at each other. Even though it is incredibly expensive, useless as a deterrent, and does nothing to solve the problems, the justice system of revenge and punishment plods on.

We do not yet have the work camps of the 1930s where single men were sent. We do not yet have the work houses of Victorian England where whole families were sent. I doubt these will appear today, just because it is so incredibly expensive. Rather we will be left to do the best we can in the inner cities of Canada.

There is another reason why the walls will probably go up to keep "us" out rather than in. The powers that be probably remember that putting single employables in work camps can have unforeseen results. In the 1930s young men herded together with nothing to do began talking with each other. Out of this came the On To Ottawa Trek, which was stopped in Regina, when the RCMP began shooting and killing them. So, all in all, the authorities have chosen the right tactic. Keep people in single rooms, isolated and depressed. It's much cheaper and does not lead to revolutions. I think I can reassure Sam who asked "Will there be camps?" that the answer is probably not.

There are, apparently, other things that people have to fear. Lately I have been seeing fearful people on television. It is February, the RRSP month. I have seen the ads of men and women sitting up in bed, going downstairs, figuring out how to go on. They are worrying if they have enough RRSPs. It is a tragedy. This country has been divided into "us" and "them," and both worlds are filled with fear.

Chapter 2
SHAME ON YOU

People are no damn good!
Motto in Minister's study
We're a burden on society

CAROL AND I WERE HAVING COFFEE one morning at McDonald's. We met there because it was across from the University of Winnipeg. After coffee she was heading across the street to sit at the CANE table at the University's "Day without Hate." The students had decided to speak up against hatred and judgment of other people. There were going to be tables set up by many groups such as women's groups, immigrant groups, aboriginal groups, etc. We were also going to have a table. Our table was going to focus on hatred against people living in poverty. This is usually called "Poor-bashing."

I was glad that Carol and some of the others were willing to sit at tables in the community. We had discovered that even such a simple thing was very hard to do. There had been a CANE table at one of the shopping malls the week before. One of our members said that she didn't know if she could sit at the table because she lived in that part of town. Some of her friends and neighbours might see her. She said "I know it's stupid, but I would be ashamed."

The shame of being poor and out of work is constant for those whom the society has decided should have paid employment. Carol and I were fifty-two and fifty-three years old. We were a part of that "lazy no-good" group of people who were not working and who were not trying hard enough to find work. As we talked we started to fantasize about how good life was going to be in a couple of years when we hit the milestone of fifty-five. Then we would both qualify for government programs such as 55 Plus money and housing, and who knew what other good things.

Then Carol started to tell me about a television show she had been watching. It was about the rise of rock and roll. One of the black singers in the early days had electrified the audience by shouting out "I'm black and I'm proud!" Carol said "Can you imagine someone today shouting out 'I'm poor and I'm proud!' " To identify oneself as non-employed and thus living in poverty is almost unthinkable.

When CANE began there were hours of discussion concerning all sorts of issues. What would we do and say, and who were we? The issue that raised the most heated debate and the issue that still occasionally arises is: What should this organization be called? We did not want to say that we were unemployed because many of us have occasional or part-time work. We wanted to create a group for people who either had no work or who had non-standard work. During a brainstorming session someone made up the word non-employed, and we had our name.

For many, the fact that we identified who we were, the non-employed, meant that they could not be a part of the group. For most people it is inconceivable that a group would call attention to the fact that they are non-employed. In our society, to be poor, to not have paid work, is to be judged and condemned. To actively announce that one is shut out of the middle class Canadian world is inconceivable.

Most of us pretend that we are still in the working world. That is one of the reasons why people living in poverty are invisible. We consciously make ourselves invisible. Those who are newly poor still have enough good working clothes to wear when they go out. Many start out in the morning in a suit and carrying a briefcase. They have no job to go to, but the image remains. One of the reasons why many refuse to call ourselves non-employed is that the role of the paid worker has to be maintained. For some of us it is possible to switch to another acceptable role. Carol and I are nearly at the age where we could call ourselves "retired." Many go back to school or training partly so they can call themselves "students." My personal favourite is what an unemployed social worker once called herself when she was presenting a brief to a committee. She said that she was "resting."

We hide ourselves by our clothes and by how we identify ourselves. Our shame is at being who we are. We know that we have been pushed off a cliff. We did not jump. The one role that we could play, and that would, in other circumstances, at least get us sympathy, would be the victim role. However, I know of very few who play this role. There would be no point. There is little sympathy from a society that believes that we just need to get up and write a better resume. Most non-employed people accept the judgment of society. They make no waves, no protests. They know that our value as persons is decided by our paid work and by our income. If we have neither, then we have no value. So we continue to walk out every morning in our work clothes, and to disappear.

For years I have been telling people without paid work that they are valuable and worthwhile people. At regular Tuesday meetings and at retreats during the year we have discussed what is happening in Canada today. The rationale for doing this is that then people will see that it is not an individual's problem, but a country's problem. People are non-employed not because they are bad and worthless, but because there is a techno-logical and a sociological revolution going on. We are just the mine canaries, the first to die. Sometimes people will listen and suddenly it makes sense. Sometimes there is a click. We will be showing the latest Statistics Canada figures, or a magazine article and someone will say "It's not me!"

The click does not always happen. Even on the tenth time, or the hundredth time it does not happen. On a Tuesday morning during discussion, once again someone will say "We're a burden on society," or "I've failed to even get an interview again." People have been programmed to consider themselves as failures, rather than to think that our country has failed to provide enough paid work for everyone.

I should not be surprised. After all it took me years to get over the shame of being a well-educated person, who is non-employed and living in poverty. For years I thought there was something the matter with me. Not only that. There was some-thing the matter with my husband. We both have university degrees and years of experience, but neither one of us could find a professional well-paying full-time job. And it was not for lack of trying. We both have stacks of rejection letters. All we could find was short-term, contract or part-time work. For years I did not know that this is the case for one quarter of the work force. For years I had accepted a false reality perpetuated by politicians and the media. We have all been told that with the right job-seeking skills and the right education or training any-one could get a job. When the job does not materialize, then we must be doing something wrong, and the cloud of failure hangs over one's life.

The feeling of guilt for not trying hard enough and shame for just not being the right kind of person has been periodically reinforced by both friends and enemies. I once heard from a friend in CANE that she had been talking to an MLA about her job search and about CANE. He told her that I did not have a job because I had a bad attitude. I had previously thought that this man was a friend. My MLA friend thinks that I am a bad person because of my bad attitude. This refers, I suspect, to my refusal to accept the rule of the market place, and my tendency to question authority. A bad habit I admit.

There are so many things to be ashamed of. One of our members told me that his mother told him that the reason he did not have a job was because he had no ambition. Our character flaws are numerous. However the condemnation most often heard is that we are not working hard enough. A letter to the editor states that "Instead of encouraging individuals to work harder, the more someone earns, the more is taken away to reward those who are less hard working."[7] The underlying assumption here is that there is only one kind of hard work - the work that is done for pay. The people I know who live in poverty are incredibly hard workers. You have to be in order to survive. Mothers at home with small children, trying to raise them with next to nothing, are the hardest workers that I know.

Possibly the person who wrote the letter meant that we are not working hard enough looking for work. I once tried to explain the employment situation to a bank manager. His response was "But are they really looking?" For many of us our days are spent constantly looking. If we do not keep looking we will be cut off welfare. This means that people no longer have any time or energy to do anything else, because constant job search means constant rejection. Many people are reminded every day of their life that they are not good enough. How long can one live under such a burden?

Although most of us by now are experts at job search, we are also assumed to be ignorant and incompetent. It is amazing to me that well-meaning people continually give us "good advice" such as "Why don't you get some help in improving your resume?" or, believe it or not "Do you check the newspapers every day?" Everybody that I know has been to at least one job-finding club, and has a beautiful resume. I know that those people with "good advice" are only trying to help us. Their intentions are good. The problem is that, for the most part, they have no idea what our lives are like, and they have no idea what would be truly helpful. Listening, without judging, would be a starting place for those who truly wish to help.

Not only do we have to deal with both friendly and professional "helpers," we also have to deal with the "blamers." The majority of people feel that it is acceptable to judge and blame us. If those of us living in poverty are there because of our defects of character, our willful ignorance or because we are just plain bad, then others feel justified in their condemnation of us. People understand that it is not acceptable to stereotype and judge others because of race, sex or disability, things that are beyond a person's control. However, it is acceptable to judge us, because we are deemed responsible for our situation, and it is just our willful perversity that keeps us in it.

We are fair game for the most heinous, hurtful judgments. Columnists can talk about "blood-sucking welfare mothers" or "those who sit at home happily living off the rest of us." It is not only those in the media, but also those in authority, such as our Prime Minister, who re-enforce the negative value judgments on people living in poverty. The Prime Minister can call those receiving Unemployment Insurance lazy, "people sitting at home drinking beer and watching television." This is considered an acceptable part of public discourse.

As Senator Erminie Cohen states, "A dilemma that poor people are facing is compounded by the fact that attitudes towards them and their plight are hardening. A new phenomena is evolving in that the poor are actively blamed by society for their own economic hardships . . . Never before have we seen this hardening of attitudes; even during the Depression years, there was relatively more public sympathy and support for those most affected by the economic downturn than there is today."[8]

The blaming, of course, goes on and on in the private conversations of thousands. The other day I was leading a workshop at a church. One of the women there said that she was a teacher and it was disgraceful the way some kids came to school, and that their mothers did not look after them. She had no idea of how mothers struggle and try and cry when they cannot feed or clothe their children. I was the only one there who defended those unknown mothers. The rest believed her. They added the story to the belief system already in place, that of unfit, uncaring welfare moms. It reminded me of a column by Margaret Wente in the Globe and Mail. The heading was "Demonizing the welfare moms." She was talking about the US where welfare mothers will be kicked off the dole after two years. "If mothers can't feed their kids, well there's always foster care, or orphanages or adoption." These moms are considered so bad that their kids should be taken away from them. Their crime is that they do not have paid work.

What struck me about the conversation with the teacher was that this was a person in one of the helping professions. What must her attitude be towards the children that she was teaching? Mind you, this was not an isolated incident. I often speak with "helpers" of various kinds. Sometimes these people identity themselves as Christians, sometimes not. Some are clergy and some are lay persons. But no matter the helper's role, the judgment is usually there.

I had a conversation with a minister the other day. This

person works with people who have no money and no hope. We were talking about the latest welfare cuts. He began to tell me how lazy and no good these people were. He had offered someone a job and this person had not taken it. Therefore, he believed that this person should be kicked off welfare. I asked what would then happen to this person. He did not care! I suggested that there may be a valid reason why this person did not take this particular job. He didn't accept that. There were to be no excuses. He looked at the people he worked with with contempt.

At first glance it seems incomprehensible. The "helpers" have become the "blamers." Not all, of course, but far too many. People living in poverty, lacking money and other resources, are too often looked down on by those who are being paid to help. In fact, research shows that people in the helping professions feel even more negative towards their clients than the general population does.[9] This happens because professional helpers are often in high stress jobs, with little positive feedback, and no control over their situation. This leads to burn out. When people become burnt out there is a shift from a positive and caring view to a negative and uncaring one.

However, the issue is broader than the burnout of some professional. Over the years there has been continual frustration of all the "helpers." As Margaret Wente writes in her previously mentioned column "The Left has been trying to improve poor people for the past fifty years, without success. The Right may have a crack at it for the next fifty years, but it will fare no better." It is indeed ironic that both the Left and the Right of the political spectrum have tried to make people good and have not succeeded. There are reasons why this is so. First, both have started from the same model of human behaviour. In our society, the individual is seen as an isolated and independent machine that can be externally motivated by reward and punishment.

The Left usually talks about "motivating" people, and the Right usually talks about "controlling" people. In both cases, external forces attempt to move the machine. In both cases, the plan is to have one billiard ball "impact" on another billiard ball in order to move it. The underlying psychological theory is called Behaviourism. What happens when the theory does not work? Neither side questions the theory. The Right's answer is to "try harder." The Right has convinced the population that we have not succeeded in making people shape up because the punishments have not been severe enough. The punishments have increased in intensity, until we are now starving people. To our great astonishment, this still is not forcing people to get a job.

The only answer must be that the machine itself is bad. This machine is a bad machine that will do bad things if you do not watch it every minute. I had a conversation the other day with someone who I know and who I like, but her view of people is as far different from mine as chalk from cheese. We were talking about our children. Everyone of my generation is at the stage where we now say "How are your kids doing?" I told her a little about my three children. At that point they were all still living at home even though they were all over twenty. Two of them were attending university. Her immediate response was that when her children were eighteen years old they would be on their own. She was quite prepared to do her duty until they were eighteen and then she felt that she was no longer responsible. I immediately questioned this approach. I know how hard it is for young people these days to find paid work. I said that my three could stay with me as long as they needed to. Then I said that we were a family. If I have a dime and one of mine needs one, then I would give it to them. Also I knew that if they had a dime and I needed it, they would give it to me. My friend said this could never work. They would exploit me. I said that she must think people are very bad if she believes that. She denied this. She said that she did not think people were bad, but that they did bad things, and that people exploited each other.

I think my friend could easily hang up on her wall the motto that we see on the minister's wall "People are no damn good."

So we have all the professional helpers who spend their lives trying to "motivate" people to do the right thing. This project is doomed to failure because everything is tainted by the underlying assumption that people are bad and must be controlled. Is it any wonder that the helpers feel like failures? The response to failure is either blaming oneself or blaming the client.

Non-professional helpers, such as friends and relations, tend to help by giving "good advice." If the person one is trying to help does not take the "good advice" then the assumption is that they "do not really want to find a job." One can then feel very self satisfied that you did all you could to help, and the non-employed person is to blame for his or her situation.

Addictive Systems

We live in a society where if anything goes wrong the response is to find out who is to blame. Talk shows are based on this premise. The whole point of most of them is to find who is to blame for the problem of the day. Then, if possible, to bring people together and to have them fling abuse at each other. Is it any wonder that helpers, either formal professional helpers, or informal friends and relations, also go back and forth between blaming themselves and blaming the person they are trying to help? The alternative is to understand that we are all caught in addictive, controlling and abusive formal structures and systems. It is very hard for people to change their perspective and to look at the system itself. In other words, it is very hard to see the forest for the trees.

The other day I was at a meeting of social workers who were struggling to come up with an action plan. One of them said "But you are criticizing social workers." No, I am not criticizing people! I am criticizing a destructive control model that has created destructive control systems. To a certain extent, people know that this is the case, but they have no understanding of the power of the systems themselves. My husband and I were once speaking to a class of Social Work students at the University of Manitoba. We spoke about our experiences over many years with the Child and Family Services system. The students agreed that the system was bad, but the problem was that there were bad people running it. The students believed that, when they became a part of the system, they would not do any of those bad things that we were talking about.

I am sure that everyone who goes into any of the helping professions feels that they are going to help, not to blame, the people that they work with. However, this surprising transformation does occur, and the harsher the system, the faster the change happens. When I worked at the old Children's Aid Society in the 1960s, we knew that the workers in the Protection Department would last two years before they would burn out. I remember that I transferred to Unmarried Parents after two years. These days some workers in Child and Family Services can only last six months because of the stress.

There have been numerous studies that show how well-meaning people turn into people who blame and control others. One of the most famous took place during WW II when British soldiers were guarding German prisoners. It was discovered that the guards were being unreasonably harsh and vindictive to the prisoners. So it was decided that they would make a complete change of guards. They would only appoint people who they felt would be fair to the prisoners. Within a few months the old problems re-appeared. The new guards were just as cruel and vindictive as the old ones.

The addictive systems that we have created abuse both the "helpers" and the "clients." Anne Schaef , in her book *The Addictive Organization: When Society Becomes an Addict,* outlines how this process operates. She points out that an addictive system is the same as an addicted individual. The system is a closed, control system. It assumes that through hard work people can become perfect. This means that one is never good enough. Other characteristics are denial of a problem, a scarcity mentality, confusion and self-centeredness. Two characteristics that are of particular interest are frozen feelings and ethical deterioration.

For many the only possible way to continue is to freeze their feelings. This is, in fact, encouraged by the system. "Helpers" are supposed to be "objective observers." For many who see how people are blamed and controlled, the only possible way to continue is to ignore the pain that the system is causing the people.

Ethical deterioration is a shift in values. For people and for systems an addictive response means that there is a loss in the ability to prioritize values. What is most valuable is no longer clear. In the case of an addictive system the values of the system itself, rather than the people it serves, have the highest priority. This was clearly illustrated to me a few years ago. My husband Robert and I had applied to be foster parents. We had previously been foster parents when our children were small. When we contacted the agency, they said there was no file on us, so we had to be assessed as foster parents. Even though I had worked for the agency in many capacities over the years, including doing foster home studies, the process had to be gone through. So we went through the assessment process and were duly pronounced acceptable. The worker phoned and told us that we would be getting a child. The next day he phoned back and said that the supervisor wanted to see us. We went into the office and there on his desk was one of the books that we had written. It is called *Empowerment: A Systems Approach to People and Groups*. The supervisor said to us "I have been reading your book. It seems to me that if there were a conflict between the interests of the agency and the interests of the child, you would do what was in the best interests of the child." We agreed. We said that the most important thing for us would be what would be most helpful to the child. He then said "Then you will never work for this agency." The agency itself is the highest priority!

All of us have to live in the destructive hierarchical control systems that we have built. It is clear that the economic system no longer has people and their well-being as its highest value. People are continually pushed out of the economic system and then are blamed because they are not able to get back in. Then we are forced into the only other alternative, the social assistance system. This blaming and the abusive social service delivery systems make the lives of most people caught in those systems a living hell.

Addicted People

The response to being caught, like a rat in a trap, is often an addictive response. The pain of always feeling ashamed of who you are leads to a variety of addictions. There are the substance addictions of alcohol, drugs, nicotine and coffee. There are the process addictions of gambling and the need for immediate gratification, which leads to "blowing the welfare cheque." Then there are the socially acceptable addictions of television watching and consumption of goods and services. Almost any substance or process can become addictive. But no matter what one chooses, the desired effect is to achieve mood control. In other words, addictive responses are ways to make one feel better.

Unfortunately, one of the effects of addiction is that people's priorities change. What was once considered valuable now has second place to the addiction. The addiction itself now becomes the most valuable thing in people's lives. In fact, people are gradually drawn to do things that would once have been totally inconsistent with their personal values.

The government actively encourages some addictive behaviours. The addiction that is newly encouraged is gambling. I became aware of how strong this addiction is while riding on the bus the other day. Two women were talking behind me. One was explaining this wonderful new opportunity. Apparently you can now get on a bus and leave Winnipeg at 9:15 at night. This bus goes to an American city. It arrives at 11:15 at night. You then can gamble until 5:00 in the morning; get on the bus; and be back in Winnipeg at 7:00 a.m. The bus is free and you get free drinks. I could not believe it! But I am sure the details are right, because the other woman kept asking questions to make sure that she understood this great new opportunity.

The private sector actively encourages other addictive behaviour. Through never-ending and constant advertising we are encouraged to drink, smoke and consume. In fact, conspicuous consumption is one of the highest values in our society. There is, fortunately, some indication that more and more people are beginning to break this addictive habit. Either people have no more money, or they understand that unlimited growth and consumption are destroying the earth. There was an article on the economic theory of shopping. One of the young girls quoted says "I never just go shopping anymore. I used to buy things to make myself feel better. Money was no object. Now I only buy things I need."[10]

There is one addiction that is not only valued, it is a sign of moral superiority - work. In *Confessions of a Workaholic*, Wayne Oates talks about work as a "religious ideal." One works hard to feel good and to be valuable. Family, community and everything else become less and less valuable.

Finally, there is the addiction enjoyed by rich and poor alike - television. It is as mind-numbing as a drug and as time-consuming as consumption or work. It reinforces other addictions through advertising. It reinforces the underlying assumptions that people are bad and need to be blamed. The numbing, dumbing effect of television addiction, or of any addiction means that we are no longer awake or alive. Our values are skewed. We are indeed sleepwalking.

A shaming and blaming society becomes an addictive society. People seek a multitude of anaesthetics and distractions to calm, for a few moments, the toxic shame of our society.

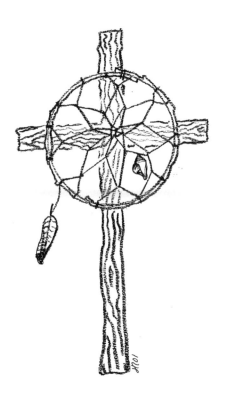

CHAPTER 3
DON'T GET YOUR
HOPES UP

Responses to job loss run the gamut; they include:
1) internalizing anger 2) adapting/adjusting 3) finding
alternative forms of income 4) creating revolt/revolution
5) rioting/looting; in Canada most people internalize their
anger and become depressed.
SHARON KIRSH, *Unemployment: Its Impact on Body and Soul*

Christmas was worse. I couldn't afford food or gifts for my
daughter. How could I tell her Santa wouldn't be here this
year . . . I wished the earth would open up and swallow me.
REALITY CHECK: *Telling our Stories of Life on Welfare in Ontario*

I T IS NOVEMBER AND THE CHRISTMAS CAROLS have started playing. I have a lot of old favourite Christmas carols. The first
Christmas record I bought forty years ago was by Andy
Williams. One of the songs starts "It's the most wonderful time
of the year." Part of me loves to play this, and I feel happy as it
brings back "memories of Christmases long ago."

There is another part of me that remembers Christmases of despair, and that knows that for many of my friends
Christmas is a horrible time of year. For those without money
there is no time more depressing than the Christmas season,
especially if you have children. It is at Christmas time that it
becomes clear how much has been lost. We stand on the out-

side of the economic system looking in. The system is a money system, and we have none. For those who ask, there is the Christmas Cheer Board's hamper available, but you have no money to buy that special gift that your child hopes that Santa will bring.

After the basic necessities are paid for there is no extra money for gifts, or for Christmas baking. If you work part-time for minimum wage, there is no extra money for Christmas. If you are receiving Employment Insurance benefits, there is no extra money for Christmas. There used to be the option of getting a small Christmas bonus from the City of Winnipeg. Then the City of Winnipeg Social Service Department changed its policy. Now you have to choose between the money, or the Cheer Board hamper. If you choose the hamper you have to phone in your request. If you have no phone (and welfare does not provide money for a phone) you have to find a free phone somewhere. Even if you find a free phone, like the one at West Broadway Community Ministry, there is a line up waiting to use it, and there is a limit to the time you can use it, and the number of the Cheer Board is always busy.

Loss of Material Things

During the rest of the year the material losses come slowly and inexorably, bit by bit. First the car goes. There is no money for gas or auto insurance. For many there is not enough money for a telephone. The small pleasures of Canadian life like a show, or eating out are no longer possible. One's diet changes gradually. For me, I always think that being poor means no pickles. Pickles are a luxury.

To my continual amazement, this loss of money, and consequently the loss of even the bare necessities, seems to be something that people with an adequate income can only grasp at a very superficial level. A number of years ago I used to be a middle class "helper." My husband, Robert, and I were teaching parenting classes in Winnipeg's inner city. One day we were talking about the things that we were thankful for. One of the mothers talked about her eldest daughter buying her the Saturday paper. She said how wonderful it felt to sit with a cup of coffee reading the paper. At the time I wondered how that simple pleasure could mean so much. Now I know.

Recently, at a meeting, I was talking to a woman about what it means to be poor. She was appalled at how low the welfare rates were. I tried to explain what this meant in practical terms. I said that those living on welfare could not even buy the paper. She thought for a moment. Then she said "Well the paper is often so biased and depressing that you don't really need to read it." She was trying to be positive about the situation. The point I was trying to make was that we do not have pickles, or papers, or anything that is not absolutely necessary. There is no disposable income.

For most of us the worst loss is the loss of one's home. Although I have not lost my home, the threat of this most terrible loss always hangs over one's head. I have seen people go from a three bedroom home to one room in a rooming house. Each move is resisted as long as possible. The pain seems worse with every move. Now many people are forced to move from a one-bedroom apartment. They thought this was the end of the line, but when you are on welfare even a one-bedroom apartment is too expensive. For more and more Canadians the end of the line is homelessness. There are now hotels full of homeless people in the "richest country in the world." In those hotels there are single mothers, desperate job seekers, addicts, old, young and those with mental health problems.[11]

In "The Street Speaks" someone has written a poem.

"We come in all colours, ages, shapes and sizes.
We are alcoholics and abstainers,
We are suffering from mental health problems
    and we are painfully sane,
We are fearful and we are fearless,
        crooked and trustworthy, atheists and true believers,
We are the homeless of your community."

Loss of Social Safety Net

It is ironic that at the same time that our country is getting richer and richer, those pushed out of the economic system are getting poorer and poorer. And the slide down to the bottom is getting faster and faster. In 1990, 87% of people who were unemployed were receiving Unemployment Insurance benefits. That number has been reduced and reduced, so that by 1995 only 48% of those unemployed were receiving Unemployment Insurance benefits.[12] Not only is it harder and harder to qualify, benefits have been reduced from 60% of a worker's former wage to 55%.

At the same time that E.I. has been reduced, the money that one receives on welfare has been reduced. In Ontario the reductions were 20%. In Manitoba the press release said that the reductions were 10%. What was not explained was that there was no reduction in the rents paid to landlords. So, in effect, the money for food and personal necessities was reduced 20%. The spin given by the government meant that the reduction did not seem as much to the average person. No one mentioned that the reduction meant that single people, who are classified as "employable" now receive $411 dollars a month in total. This is for rent, food, clothing, personal needs, everything.

It was only those who were affected who realized what

---

had happened, and our outcry does not get much media. Ever since that horrible day of the 20% welfare cut to people's food, clothing and personal needs, CANE has had a vigil once a month entitled "The Government is Starving the People." We do not get much media coverage. One day a CBC radio reporter phoned and asked about it, because we do periodically send out News Releases. She later got back to me, and said that the editor had told her they had already covered the story. I know that they had not. No CBC radio reporter had ever contacted us about the vigil.

Although I definitely believe that it makes a difference which political party one supports, when it comes to welfare policy no political party has been better than another. Those at the bottom live in destitution no matter which political party is in power. A few years ago, when I was on the National Anti-Poverty Organization Board of Directors, the board met in Regina. We met with the NDP Government of Saskatchewan. We pointed out that the welfare rates were the same in their province as they were in Conservative Manitoba. The response was silence.

Loss of Rights

For most people existing on either federal, provincial or municipal social programs, the focus is on how to survive today and tomorrow. They experience the cuts, but do not connect them to another hidden loss, the loss of our rights as Canadian citizens. When the Federal Liberal government eliminated the Canada Assistance Plan, and substituted the Canada Health and Social Transfer, there was a loss of $7 billion dollars to the provinces. However, more than money was lost. Within the C.A.P. legislation there were five basic rights. These were: the right to assistance; the right to an adequate amount of assistance; the right to appeal; the right not to be forced to work or train for assistance; and the right as a Canadian citizen to receive assistance regardless of the province you lived in. Only one of these rights was put into the new legislation. There was to be no residency requirement for assistance. For a time, even this right was denied people living in BC. However, it has since been reinstated.

The effect of this legislative change by the federal government was a green light to the provinces to cut programs, to reduce benefits, and to instigate workfare. Provincial governments now had someone else to blame for cuts they made. Health and welfare cuts would have caused an uproar, but massive cuts could be made in social services with very little risk to their popularity. In Manitoba the cuts were not even debated in the legislature. They were made by Order-in-Council. A group of men and women sat around a table and decided to beggar their fellow citizens. Canadians without work are despised, blamed and punished on a regular basis. I suspect that most people on assistance do not realize that they have lost the legal rights they once had to survive. All they know is that they, and their children, are getting hungrier and hungrier.

Loss of Relationships

At the same time that one's physical losses are piling up, one experiences the loss of family and friends. As you slip out of the economic system, you also slip out of the old relationships you had. Co-workers no longer are a part of your life. For a while you go out for lunch or coffee with them, but eventually there is no money left for this extravagance. I have a few friends that will take me out for lunch. Oh what bliss this is! You go to a restaurant, and are able to order what you want, and you eat it without a knot in your stomach as you worry about what you will have to go without this month in order to pay the bill.

For some there is also the loss of their religious community. For most of my life I have belonged to the United Church community. This church is essentially a middle class institution. The prayers and hymns and sermons have nothing to do with the world I now live in. Prayers of confession usually ask God to forgive us for not doing enough to "help" the poor. At first I thought that maybe I was being too critical of the church community. But one day I talked to a minister on the United Church regional staff. She told me that she had been involved in taking some poor people on a weekend retreat. She had been unable to find any prayers, hymns, or stories that related to their lives.

For the most part those of us living in poverty tend to withdraw from our friends, family and church community. The reason for this withdrawal is the constant pain of saying "No, I haven't found work yet; no, I don't need another update of my resume; and yes, I have thought about checking the want ads in the paper." Yes, people do ask such questions. All the questions are well-meaning, but all imply that there is something wrong with our job-finding skills, our resumes, or just who we are as people. It is also implied that if we "really" tried and were well-qualified, then we would have a job.

From personal experience, and from the literature,[13] I know that attacks are launched by family and friends. Family members and close friends feel the unemployed are not working hard enough at finding work. In order to survive emotionally, we have to build defences to protect ourselves. The defence for most of us is to withdraw. Surely it is a rational thing to do to attempt to escape pain. The pain and despair of explaining that there is no job at a living wage for one and a half million of us, defeats us. Withdrawal from the questions may isolate us further, but the questions push us further into despair.

Loss of Hope

Depression means that you are tired all the time. We have less and less energy to do even the basics. One day last winter a bottle broke on our front steps. I did not have the energy to clean it up. After a week the lady who delivered the paper cleaned it up. We have since stopped the paper. My energy level has risen, but only on good days do I have enough energy to cook from scratch or to work on this book.

It is more than being tired. It is the sense that it is impossible to do anything to change your situation. Something monstrous has happened to you even though you have done your best. And it seems that no one cares.

One of our members wrote an article for our newsletter explaining what it is like. He called it "Give a dog a bone."

"I grew up on a small southern Ontario farm by the Owen Sound Road. It was a busy thoroughfare, and we children often found lost or abandoned items beside it. Too often I can remember seeing people dump a dog, "no longer wanted on the voyage," on the roadside near our gate, usually on a Saturday. Someone would push the castaway out of the vehicle and before the dog knew what was happening the car would disappear in a cloud of dust.

With our parents' blessing and Pavlovian haste, we would approach the outcast and try to lure it home. There would be no way that we could get it to come. It would eat and drink what we brought. It would not quit its vigil. For days the dog would pace up and down vainly looking for signs of its owners. It would believe to its dying day that its owners would return.

Early in 1991 I was told I would be laid off at the end of the year. In the years since then, I have paced the information highway up and down, firing unanswered salvos of applications by fax, phone and mail, hoping a new or former employer would take me on, and I sense a growing close bond with the castoff curs of yesteryear."

The classic experiment in artificially created depression was performed by Martin Seligman.[14] The experiment was done with dogs. A dog was placed in a cage and electric shocks were administered. The dog would attempt to escape, but the cage was designed so that no matter what the dog did, it could not get out. After a while, it just lay down and stopped trying. The experimenters then opened the cage door. The dog did not jump up and run out of the cage. It continued to lie there, being shocked, without hope.

The Professional "Helpers"

No one is permitted to lie down in despair. We have to get up, and keep working at our job. We are told that our job is looking for work, and we are condemned to keep at this job for the rest of our lives. However, we will not be left alone. We are trapped in a world of professional "helpers" and their questions, comments and advice can not be ignored. In fact, we are compelled to sit and listen to them if we want to continue eating. There is now no escape from the job-finding "helpers" of government bureaucracies. Programs that used to be freely chosen are now compulsory.

At its simplest, job-finding clubs, either public or private, use some variation of the "carrot and stick" brand of motivation. If you believe that people are machines and that they can be made to do what they are told, then job-finding clubs are perfectly logical. The carrot that leads one on is some variation of "You too will find a job if you have a positive attitude." The Canada Employment Centre book "How to Find a Job" asks "Is your attitude holding you back? Be confident and assertive." This reflects all job-finding conventional wisdom. The problem that is totally discounted is that we are all depressed.

Occasionally the problem of the depressed job seeker is addressed. One of our members who is forced to go to a job-finding club challenged the idea that it was possible to be positive all the time. The person leading the group then talked about how we could give ourselves little treats. She suggested that one could have a nice long bubble bath. When you do not have enough to eat it is hard to imagine buying bubble bath so you can have a better attitude.

Jamie Swift talks about the job-finding clubs in Windsor, Ontario.[15] One club is like an Alcoholics Anonymous meeting. People introduce themselves, describe their situations and their feelings about being unemployed. Then the negative feelings are identified as the reason why the person does not have a job. All negative feelings are to be denied. Only positive feelings, feelings of self-confidence and enthusiasm are accepted.

People that encourage "the positive attitude" are usually well meaning, and believe this is the answer. Even religious communities can believe in the power of positive thinking. I, and a number of CANE members, once went to a retreat given by a religious community. We were a third of the group. There was lots of food and fun, as well as small group sessions to share with each other. Issues such as loss and the "ripple effect" of unemployment were discussed. During the week-end it became clear that people were in very different stages of loss. Some had only been unemployed for a few months. Some had been unemployed for years. However, we all could listen and support each other.

At the final session of the retreat we were invited to share community resources with each other. On the table were resources such as "How to Write a Resume." People began to talk about helpful job-finding clubs they were involved in. All the old clichés and helpful advice were trotted out in the hope that we would leave feeling positive about our job search. Fortunately, or unfortunately, the members of CANE who were there started to talk about the reality we were entering. Some of us had been looking for work for five, six, or ten years. Some of us had professional degrees. All of us had marketable skills. We began to say that having a positive attitude was a good thing, but it did not necessarily mean we would find a job. The response from the leaders and some of the others was anger at us for implying that we would not necessarily get work. It is now a year later, and some of those people are beginning to come to CANE. Some probably got a job and some are probably back in despair.

What I and the others were trying to say to the people at the retreat was "beware of the emotional roller-coaster." The job-finding clubs are a part of the emotional roller-coaster we have all ridden. You walk into one at a point of depression, and you are taken up the roller-coaster to enthusiasm, and confidence, and then are sent out to get a job. I have listened to many people who have come out of job-finding clubs. They are always pumped up and always say things like "I am really going to get serious about my job search. This time I am really going to find work." If you are one of those who do not find work, the emotional low point, the trough, is deeper this time. Every time you get on the roller-coaster, the bottom is lower. The end of the ride can be fatalism, burn-out and despair.

The other major reason for the despair is that people are taught that they and they alone are responsible for their situation. In the Windsor Help Centre, the "helper" who runs it "cracks the whip." He says "the onus is on you; you are responsible." He also says what all job-finding clubs say "Get out there and sell yourself." We are all to be salesmen and saleswomen and the product is ourselves.

If people are individually responsible for their situation, and if they do not find a job, then the answer of the social service bureaucracies is to bring out the stick. It is an emotional stick. We are not yet as merciless as the US with our sticks, but it is coming. The other day one of our members was shown a documentary from 60 Minutes on a US job-finding club in Harlem, called Strive. People were yelled at and browbeaten. When the clients in the Winnipeg club were asked what they thought, half of them thought this was a good idea. After all, if we are bad and lazy, we deserve to be yelled at.

The browbeating, intimidation and bullying is not limited to job-finding clubs. If one is trapped in the welfare system, then this negative attitude can be encountered any time one has to deal with the system in any way. One of our members heard a worker talking on the phone to a client. It was obvious that the client was asking for money for a winter coat. She was told "You live in Winnipeg. You knew winter was coming. Why didn't you save up for it?" The fact that one does not get enough money to have an adequate diet is discounted. After surveying a number of people we have found that getting money for a winter coat is totally arbitrary. There are no rules that we can find. It depends on whether your worker likes you or has had a good day.

One of our members was in the welfare office the other day. She had been waiting a long time to see her worker. Finally, as it was past lunch time, she asked how much longer it would be. The receptionist looked at her and said "You look like you could skip a meal." Where else would people be treated with such disrespect?

"There is nothing the welfare client can do within the context of his dependent condition that merits respect... adaptation must take place leading either to re-definition of self and adoption of alternative values, or to some individual form of escape from his situation, or to the acceptance of defeat."[16]   It is no wonder that the combination of no job, no money and being treated as though one is less than human leads to clinical depression. Technically it is called "situation depression," or, depression caused by external circumstances. I also know what the answer to this depression is believed to be.

The Professional Answer

I sometimes play the part of a patient in order to make a few dollars. I have a friend who works for the General Practice section of the School of Medicine. Part of the exams for medical students is to examine people who pretend to have various illnesses. One day I was called upon to play the part of a forty-five year old woman, who worked for the federal government, and who was afraid that she would lose her job. Her problem was depression. After I auditioned to play this part, one of the doctors said "Gee, you really play that part well. I really could sense how depressed you were." She thought I was a wonderful actor. It wasn't a hard part to play. I know exactly how such a person would feel. I also know exactly how this person would feel after she did lose her job.

The day I was a patient I sat in a room, and one by one

young doctors came in and interviewed me. They were to find out how I was feeling and why. Then they were to prescribe the acceptable treatment. The right answer was to prescribe drugs. More and more of our members are on drugs. It is not apparent at first. I did not realize this until, as the months went by and I got to know more and more people, I heard more and more talk about medication. People would hold out as long as possible and then drugs would be offered and taken.

The Last Answer

Whether one is on drugs or not the roller-coaster ride continues. Job searching continues. You go to the job-finding club to "get pumped up." Then you start looking, sending out resumes. "I sent out twenty-five resumes in one week, and not one response. I was so depressed. They never even call." Last week I talked to a teacher, who said that she was no longer applying for permanent jobs. She could no longer take the emotional toll of constant rejection. If you persist, and you get an interview, there is a brief feeling of hope. But the interview may not be all you wish it was.

> "The longer I was out of work, the harder it was to give a good job interview. It was painful to hear myself, sounding unsure, an edge of pleading in my voice."[17]

> "It makes you feel inadequate. The longer it goes on, the worse it gets."[18]

> "It seems there's always a little lower you can go, a little more horror just around the corner." [19]

> "I find myself sometimes thinking we'd be better off

dead . . . I must fight this depression caused by the stress I am under, but it is becoming more difficult every day to remain calm."[20]

The final solution for some is suicide. It may be an act of deliberate destruction, or it may just be a giving up of life. The body just closes down, and there is no longer the will to live.

Christmas 1995

I have never contemplated suicide, but I have known despair. The low point in my journey took place December 22, 1995. I recorded it, because I did not want to forget what we as a people do to our neighbours.

We walked into the Welfare Appeal Board office - the crusader for justice, and a nineteen year old who had been cut off welfare because he had not answered a phone call. The phone call had been left on his friend's answering machine. The friend was my son, and both boys swear they never received such a call. Was the call left? We will never know. But I walked in confident in the basic justice and caring of Canadians. It was inconceivable that someone would be left on the street to die because he had not returned a phone call, and was thus labeled non-cooperative. I had seen the form. The reason he was denied welfare, was because he was non-cooperative.

Thinking about it later I still could not believe what happened in that office. I had been sure that everything would be all right. Yes, I knew how mean-spirited the system is. After all every day I listened to the stories and heard the pain. But I was still that one step away from it happening to me. Now it has, and I pray I never forget that moment of utter humiliation as I wept before the appeal board, and begged them to give my son's friend some money to live, some acknowledgment that he did in fact have a right to live.

The process began on a low-key rational note. Here we were appealing. Here was the lawyer from the City of Winnipeg welfare department. Here were three judges, impartial judges we were told, that would decide whether he would be re-instated. The lawyer began by showing the boy the list of his crimes against the system, a list that we had not seen until we sat down. I am not a lawyer, but my first thought was that the accused should have the right to see the charges against him before the trial. Apparently not.

The list of crimes were all crimes of non-cooperation. I remembered some of them. One day he had not been home when a temporary agency had called about a job. He had been on his way to the welfare office to pick up his cheque. He was now told that he should have known that he was always to be available, and that going to pick up your cheque was not an excuse. This crime, like most of the others involved the telephone. As I listened I tried to put this together with the fact that on welfare no one is given money for a telephone. He was being condemned because he was not responding to telephone calls on my son's phone.

The trial then shifted to how many job applications he had submitted in the last month. The judge now became the prosecutor. She badgered him for details. We all knew that he had done little. He was at the stage of frustration and despair. At this point I joined the discussion in an attempt to help him. I pointed out to the judge/prosecutor that there were 44,000 people actively looking for work in Manitoba last month and there were 6,000 fewer jobs available than there had been the month before. I was then turned on as the enemy, told that this was irrelevant, and felt the full force of the righteous indignation of those chosen to root out the unworthy of our society. I could then sense the judge/prosecutor putting on the black hat in order to pronounce sentence.

At that point I was overwhelmed by our powerlessness. This young man, whom I had known since he was in Grade Three, was to be pronounced guilty of non-cooperation. He would no longer be given money to live. He could go out and die on the street. The system would condemn him to be cast out with no rights, and the system would maintain that no one was responsible. I put down my head and wept. It was two days before Christmas, and Herod was killing the children again.

Christmas 1997

There are many kinds of despair and hopelessness. Being excluded from the world we once knew when we were ordinary working Canadians, and having no acceptable new world to step into can leave one totally alone. This experience is intensified at Christmas. Family and friends might be physically there, but they are in one world and you are in another. They are in the world of presents and chocolates and maybe wine, and going to shows and out for supper. There is no room for Christmas in the other world.

There appears to be some recognition of despair at

Christmas this year. Some of the churches have held Blue Christmas services. I went to a couple. The pain of hopelessness and loss of many different kinds was shown in one service by the extinguishing of a candle. In another service it was shown by the lighting of a candle.

If I had been planning the service I might have used the image of a box with no way out. We live in boxes where the walls have no windows, and the locked doors have no keys. At least, that is how we see life. We believe our boxes have no way out because we are told that this is reality. We are told that nothing can be done. Those with power in the political arena, or in the bureaucratic institutions that govern our lives, tell us there is no choice. No hope means no choice, and no way out.

How long can one stay in The Box of No Choice? Some explode in anger and violence and some lie down and die. Some just put one foot in front of the other and keep going, head down and eyes full of tears, and some blot out the world with one addiction or another. These are the choices of the despairing.

On bad days I lay my head down and cry. But that is not how I choose to go on. For we are free to choose. No one, no group, no institution can take that away from us. I can choose to join with others, and plant seeds that will grow. I can dance with others in the darkness. I can choose to believe that it is better to light one candle than to curse the dark.

Chapter 4
ANGER and VIOLENCE

The Sydney violence illustrates the frustration of many Canadians unable to find work.
Finance Minister Paul Martin,
Toronto Star, March 2, 1997

The eff'n mayor should spend an eff'n night at the D.I. (Calgary Drop-In), then things might get better.
The Street Speaks

A T THE TOP OF THE ESCALATOR in the Winnipeg Centennial Library there is usually a list of Vision TV listings, which often contain National Film Board productions. One day I read the list and saw an NFB video listed which dealt with unemployment in the 1980s. I took the video out of the library and went home and watched it. For an hour I watched people telling their stories. One after another, Canadian men and women spoke about what it was like to be unemployed, to be poor, to have no hope in the future. It was nothing new. I heard stories like this every day at CANE. After a while you just accept this as Canada today. But I did not know the people on the tape. There were new stories I had not heard before. As I watched I felt worse and worse. The injustice of the systems, and the fact that nobody seems to care hit me again. That is what it feels like - a punch in the gut.

What do we do when someone punches us? Some of us

punch back. Our bodies even get ready to fight. Physical changes take place. There is an increased heart and pulse rate and a tightening of the muscles. The angrier we are, the more our bodies react. I have occasionally felt physically sick with rage at a person or a situation. Now, as I sat and watched the film, I felt my body beginning to tense. The process was starting. My response to injustice had been programmed long ago. My response was encouraged by my culture and my temperament. I knew where the response was taking me. I would be left feeling powerless against seemingly overwhelming forces. I had felt that too often. My pain for those who were suffering was real and powerful. My response of anger was a choice I no longer wished to make. I chose to re-dedicate my life to the cause of non-employed people. I recognized that what I was doing had value. To my great joy I felt a sense of both peace and power.

The process that I went through confirmed for me what only a few writers and researchers have concluded. June Crawford and her colleagues have found that "anger was not empowering, rather it was a passion that overcomes us as a response of powerlessness...if you are powerful, you have no need to be angry."[21] This position is contrary to the "common sense" of our culture.

Questioning "Common Sense"

Someone once told me that I was always questioning things. It was meant as a compliment, and I took it as such. I began to question anger as an appropriate response a long time ago. When my husband and I taught parenting courses in Winnipeg's inner city, the first thing we discovered was that parents were overwhelmed by their negative feelings. There was a never-ending cycle of fear/blame/despair/anger. Parents spent their lives going from one state to another in this cycle. We would diagram this cycle and get them to identify where they were and had been that week. Every one of them would immediately identify with this negative feeling circle. The reaction to it is not limited to parents struggling to cope with their children. We showed the diagram to a friend who did not have any children and he said "That's my life."

It became clear that for parents any one of the four negative feelings inevitably led to all of them. In order for parents to survive emotionally they needed to find a way to experience alternative emotional states. We quickly identified faith as the opposite of fear, forgiveness as the opposite of blame and hope as the opposite of despair. It was not clear what the opposite of anger was. We could never find a word that crystallized the exact opposite. The closest we came to it was peaceful strength. Ten years later, as I began to look at anger again in relationship to social justice issues I discovered that we were not the only ones who had trouble identifying a clear and precise opposite feeling to anger. Thomas Aquinas listed eleven passions with only anger having no opposite.

Not only is there no precise word to identify the opposite of anger, there is also an overwhelming desire by most people to praise anger as a "good thing." We live in a society that says that anger is a good and appropriate response, when used in a positive constructive way. So many writers and leaders have said that anger is empowering, or that anger can be a motivating force. The baseball father yells at his son at bat to "get mad." A children's book teaches that anger can motivate you to change things for the better. Respected theologians counsel us to claim anger as a virtue, even though it was once considered one of the Seven Deadly Sins. People think the response of anger is required when one faces injustice at any level. In fact the theologian Robert McAfee Brown says there is something wrong with us if we are not angry when we see starving children. On the other hand smaller injustices produce the same response. People get mad when someone cuts them off in a line at the grocery store. And people get really mad if someone in another car cuts them off.

So why don't I just accept anger as natural, and focus on how to "manage" anger, as most of the experts suggest? I can't accept it because the more I got involved with justice issues for the society as a whole and justice for myself and my family, the angrier I got. It was not until I started to really think about this, and watch myself getting angry that I began to realize that I no longer wanted to live the emotional life of continuous rage with the accompanying emotions of fear, blame and despair. I was determined to see if an alternative was possible.

The process was a gradual one and began as I recognized that my anger was getting out of control. One day I was at a large meeting called by Winnipeg City Councillor Glen Murray. The room was filled with people concerned with poverty issues. We were encouraged to brain storm and throw out ideas around what could be done. There was a long list of things suggested. I thought that most of them would never be done because no one seemed willing to commit their time and energy to one of the suggested projects. My frustration level was rising. I had heard all this before. Then a young single mom on welfare suggested a walk-a-thon to raise money. I angrily said that this would not solve the problems we were facing. There was no excuse for my angry outburst. I apologized to her later, but the damage had been done. Three years of frustration at trying to do something constructive had boiled over in a totally inappropriate way. I had not realized how angry I was.

Over the years I have responded in anger to those who were not doing enough, or who were using the wrong strategy, or who were not sufficiently aware of the problems. In one meeting of social activists, whose purpose was to be a supportive group for those struggling for justice, one participant said how discouraged and burnt out she and many others were. I responded by saying angrily that she at least had enough to eat.

The last time I was aware of how destructive my anger could be was when I ran into an old social worker friend of mine. We began talking about the difference in the Social Work profession between the 1960s and today. When I was a newly graduated social worker in 1967 there were twenty five people on the Social Action Committee of the Manitoba Association of Social Workers. Now there is my friend Bonnie and I. The whole social safety net has been ripped apart, and there is no response from those who see every day the suffering of thousands. As I talked I became madder and madder. But I caught myself and stopped. My friend began to talk about how hard it was to work in the social work field, and how overwhelmed she felt. The conversation then switched to happier topics, such as what our children were doing now. I hope that if I meet her again she will not run away from me because she does not want to deal with my anger.

Whether the anger is directed at our "friends" or our "enemies," the cause is the same. People are not doing what we want them to do. Anger comes when we feel powerless and unable to control other people or situations, and therefore we feel unable to reach the goals that matter to us. The goal may be a job for oneself or social justice for everyone. The goals we seek can be as basic as having enough food to eat, or as frivolous as dinning on champagne and caviar, and whatever else the rich assume they need. When our goals are blocked by outside causes, we say that the outside causes "make me angry."

The vast majority of the literature on anger and violence

focuses on finding out the causes of anger and the causes of violence. The book *Violence and the Media* is subtitled "The Question of Cause and Effect." This book, by Victoria Sherrow, looks at a multitude of causes and concludes that no single condition or influence has brought about all the violence around us. This is the same conclusion reached by *Television and the Aggressive Child: The Gross National Comparison*. The editors point to culture, environment, parental norms and personal characteristics. The experts agree that there is no one cause of anger and violence. They tend to outline the multiplicity of causes. Given this cause and effect model of how the world works, the causes tend to fall into three categories: mean people, mean world, and the media.

MEAN PEOPLE

One day in the library I found a book for children on how to cope with anger. One of the exercises was to first ask oneself "Who makes me angry?" A list of possible suspects was given: parents, teachers, siblings, etc. We are taught that the people around us are responsible for our anger, because they are doing bad things. As we grow up we gradually add more and more people to the list, and soon we live our lives surrounded by bad mean people.

Who are these bad people? They are both individuals whom we know, and those whom we do not know. We also judge whole groups of people. Everyone seems to have some group of people who are the bad people. There are, of course, those in the society who have been legally judged as bad, and have been sentenced by the courts. Amazingly, there are millions more bad people out there. For some those on welfare are bad, and usually they are called "lazy bums." For some, those in unions are bad, and they are called "greedy." And, of course, bank presidents and CEOs are generally called bad, and they too are called "greedy."

Unfortunately, even those who suffer the most join in the witch hunts to find and punish the bad people. The other day I answered the phone in the CANE office. A young man, who was unemployed, had been given our number by his MLA's office. I was not sure what he wanted or how I could help him. So I just listened to his pain and anger at life. He had experience, and had worked hard at his former jobs, and now he could not get work of any kind. He described how he had put resumes in everywhere, and had even sometimes gotten an interview. Life was incomprehensible to him. Why did he not have work? I began to explain that this situation was not his fault, and to suggest some of the larger societal causes for his lack of work. It soon became obvious that he was not interested in my explanations. He had already decided what the problem was. It was immigration, particularly immigration from the Philippines. He believed the government got "them" jobs, and would not help him, even though he was a Canadian. His anger was focused on government and immigrants. He had found his bad people. Nothing I could say would change his mind.

I have exactly the same emotional response towards government as the man on the phone, but for different reasons. In my role as chairperson of CANE, I was constantly in the presence of politicians of one stripe or another. For example, I was at the hearings in Manitoba on the Calgary Declaration. I was sitting beside a Conservative cabinet minister. During the break we began to talk. She said that she thought she recognized me from United College (now the University of Winnipeg). We figured out that we had indeed attended during the same years. The conversation switched to today. It soon became clear that her views were diametrically opposed to mine. She really believed that there were enough jobs for everyone in the society, and that we were just being too picky, and not willing to take anything. Statistics and research meant nothing to her. She based her beliefs on her life experience. She had worked her way through university twenty-five years ago, and she did not see why the young people today could not do the same. I was so mad I could hardly be civil to the woman. Here was a woman who had cut welfare rates and programs, and who had brought in workfare, and she was blaming the people who were now suffering because of her actions. I felt rage at her complacent arrogance.

The last time that I felt such a feeling of powerless rage was in the Manitoba Court of Appeal. I knew from previous experiences that the Welfare Appeal Board is comprised of people appointed by the government, whose main function is to deny appeals. But I did not think that the provincial courts would deny someone simple justice. The role of the courts in this case was simply to rule whether or not the applicant could appeal a welfare decision.

The case seemed a simple one. Alan Maki is a political refugee from the United States. He and his family have been living in the Rural Municipality of LaBroguerie since 1990. He began the process for refugee status, and then discovered that while the application was being processed he was forbidden to work. Thus he was forced to apply for welfare. The welfare rules state that he must have residency, and that he must be available for work and seeking work. Because he was not eligible to work by Federal Court Order, the municipality refused to give him assistance because he was not seeking work. One level of government refused to allow him to work; the other level of government refused him assistance. Maki, his wife and the CANE members in the court felt justice would be given in this Catch 22 situation. We were wrong. The request to appeal the welfare decision was denied. There was a stunned silence in the courtroom.

Helpless rage engulfed me. It was only by the greatest act of will that I did not stand up and say words that I probably would have regretted. I now realize that these times of powerful anger occur when I am confronted by the powers in our society as represented by judges and politicians. When we feel the most powerless, then we feel the most angry. And I feel most powerless when I am struggling not only against individuals, but against the legal, political and economic systems, the mean world, out there.

MEAN WORLD

There is a "mean world syndrome."[22] The United States was described by the United States' Senate Judiciary Committee in 1991 "as the most violent and self-destructive nation on earth." The US culture has been described and analyzed by countless experts. Willard Gaylin writes about the anger of the average US citizen.[23] He says to walk the streets of a typical US city is to see anger everywhere. The anger is expressed by those shut out of the economic system. The social response to this anger is jail and execution. Incarceration is so prevalent that in California one-third of the black male population is involved in the justice system at some level. The ante has just recently been upped by enacting the three-strikes-you-are-out law. This has resulted in a man going to jail for life for stealing a piece of pizza. How fitting that one of the most popular musicals today is about a man going to jail for years for stealing a loaf of bread. We have now returned to 17th century France.

Writers from the United States are now making a connection between the individual violence that is so prevalent, and the violence done to people by the mean economic system. The current economic system is so mean to so many that the writer Charles Derber compares it to the violent crime of "wilding." Wilding is a term meaning random violence by youth gangs. He says the individualistic competitive culture of the United States has become a license for unrestrained and sociopathic self-interest. Economic wilding is the morally uninhibited pursuit of money. It has led to crises such as the savings and loan collapse in the United States. It has led us to globalization where big business has the entire Third World as its reserve army of cheap labour.

In Canada, the anger and violence has not yet reached the same level as in the United States. There are some counterbalancing forces that have so far prevented us from becoming exactly like our neighbours. We have not totally internalized the myth of the US frontier. This myth idealizes rugged individualism, where conflicts are settled by a shoot out between the guys in the white hats and those in the black hats. Fortunately, in Canada we have strict gun control laws. Not only that, we have the myth of the Mounties riding in to settle disputes. This myth is reflected in our constitution. The federal government is empowered to see that we have "Peace, order and good government."

We also have been fortunate to have a tradition of the commons, shared space and shared resources. We spent years building a social safety net so that all our citizens would live in a "kinder gentler nation." Unfortunately, the nation called Canada has now torn the net apart in a rush to be competitive in the global marketplace. We have accepted this view of economics, and ignored the consequences. We have accepted the resulting poverty and the widening gap between the rich and the poor as inevitable and unchangeable. We have accepted a meaner and meaner world for more and more of our citizens. And only occasionally has there been a violent response to this violent economic upheaval.

One example happened in Sydney, Nova Scotia. In March 1997 a building was burned; firefighters were prevented from quelling the fire; and security guards were roughed up. The headline of the article in the Toronto Star was "Anger spills over as jobless rate is highest in country." This was only one incident. However, the federal government now sees the possibility of angry people becoming violent. "Feds fear violence when TAGS aid ends."[24] As the program to compensate Atlantic fishers for the loss of the fisheries was about to end the reaction of the government was to spend $350,000 dollars training officials to deal with "potentially serious, life-threatening situations." However, being Canadians the examples mentioned are demonstrations and sit-ins. So far the workers' response has been as the government predicted, and there has been no actual violence. In April 1998 there was a lock-out at a taxation office in Newfoundland because the TAGS program was ending.

There are, however, some things that are the same in both Canada and the United States. In both countries we live as isolated individuals, whose lives are governed by huge bureaucracies. Today both government services and private business are usually bureaucratic. It is the way we structure all the institutions in our society. The rules are the rules, whether public or private. And the rules for those not in the market economy are the meanest of all.

I thank God that I have been able to stay out of the clutches of the Canadian welfare system. As it has become harder and harder to qualify for EI benefits, more and more Canadians find themselves caught in a system that neither knows, nor cares, who you are. No one cares if you live or die. More and more people are cut off the welfare system, and God knows what happens to them. There is no record. If you do not "cooperate," if you do not do your required job search, you no longer have a right to receive money to live.

You are told what to do, and the rules around job search become meaner and meaner. For example, you can only submit an application if the business is looking for someone. You can only apply to ten stores in a mall. So in Winnipeg, in the winter, you are forced out onto the streets. And you may or may not be given money for a bus pass. You may or may not be given money for a winter coat. There are rules that force you into slavery, but there are no rights that permit you to live in dignity.

We in mainstream white Canadian culture are just beginning to experience a totally controlled life of slavery. Our Aboriginal brothers and sisters have experienced this for generations. The response of Aboriginal peoples has been despair, addiction and violence. Native peoples have more often reacted with violence towards themselves than with violence towards their oppressors. Ovide Mercredi, former National Chief of Assembly of First Nations has said that native suicides can be traced directly to the lack of economic opportunities for native peoples.[25]

Alma Brooks, an elder on St. Mary's Reserve near Fredericton is quoted as saying "These reserves have been like a prison. As long as we keep our mouths shut, and kill ourselves, everybody is happy." In New Brunswick Aboriginal peoples are fighting for the right to cut trees on Crown land. For the first time in decades they have work and money and they are not willing to go back to subsistence living in an oppressive system. To our great shame, there are still few opportunities for Aboriginal peoples, particularly young people. We are now seeing the violence expanding to the wider community. In BC young

Aboriginal peoples are increasingly turning to violence and crime out of frustration with racism, unemployment and long-standing unresolved land claims. In the last year minor crimes have doubled and serious offences almost tripled.[26]

MEDIA

It is not only Aboriginal young people that are lashing out in violent behaviour. I can understand the rage of the teenagers who smashed all the windows in my son's fancy sports car. I must confess that a few years ago, when things were very dark, and there seemed no alternatives possible, I would look at the fancy sports cars in the parking lot beside our house and feel like smashing all the windows. Some days we look out at the world and believe that there is only pain and suffering. There is poverty and injustice and bad people doing bad things. The media takes this vision of the world and expands and amplifies it. The media then gives us the two standard acceptable responses. There is flight or fight. Escape into the media world of soap operas and game shows is flight. Anger, leading to the fight response, is encouraged by the black and white world of villains and heroes where the heroes always win.

No discussion on anger and violence would be complete without looking at the impact of the media. The media constantly present us with situations and people in a way that deliberately tries to evoke an angry response. As Phil Donahue would say after he had considered an issue, "Doesn't it make you angry?" Some studies say that the media cause the violence, and some studies say that the media reflect the society we live in. I believe that the media do not just reflect our society, as a mirror does. The media amplify what is already happening.

One night I was watching Pamela Wallin on Newsworld. She was interviewing a writer named Deborah Tanner. Tanner is an expert on communication. She was talking about how we demonize people, and how the media have an "ethic of aggression." In every issue the media seek out the two polarized sides. They set up a "black hat" and a "white hat" to fight it out. Tanner talked about the confrontational approach to problem-solving as part of our Western culture. We assume that this is natural, not cultural. A simple example is that in North America if two cars are in a collision, both drivers jump out and accuse each other of being at fault. This may escalate into one, or both, going to court to prove that the other is to blame. In Japan if two cars collide both drivers jump out, bow, and apologize to each other. In Western culture we believe that there is a right and a wrong side to every issue. To apologize would mean that one was in the wrong, and that would be intolerable. The media have taken the way of confrontation as a means of seeking the truth, and have developed it into an automatic ritual opposition. We now feel that this is the only way to deal with problems. People feel they have to attack. People feel angry all the time.

Our angry feelings are encouraged by the continual fighting and confrontation over every issue, but it is more than the content of our media that is the problem. There has always been violence, fighting and anger in our literature, whether great books or comic books. But now in the Communication Age our new technologies mean that more and more of our senses are engaged. When TV is the medium we add an audio, and a fast action visual dimension, to what was visual but static. Then computer games and CD-Roms add another dimension. Virtual reality games are another step. Adults and children now do not just watch people being shot. They do the shooting. Now we have the Internet and electronic mail. Tanner points out that this latest technology "ratchets up" our ability to rage at other people. Other people are now anonymous, unknown. It becomes easy to attack another verbally because you do not have to see them. They are not human, just mechanical.

Not everyone has a computer, but most people have a television set. The interconnectedness of the violent words on the TV talk shows, and the violence in the cop shows, and the violence in the news, and the violence in the streets is a source of continual speculation and study. There are books and books, and studies and studies on violence and the media. According to the American Psychiatric Association there is more published research on how media violence affects people than on almost any other social issue of our times.

There are two points of general agreement. First, both violence on TV, and in other media, and violence in the society have steadily risen. Secondly, there is general agreement that before age eight or nine children cannot distinguish between fantasy and reality on the screen. They do not know what "real blood" and "real death" means. Therefore if they are immersed in the television world they grow up in a mean, scary place even it their personal world is a safe and caring place. As a society we are just beginning to accept all the studies that show there is a correlation between the amount of violent television watched by children before age nine, and their degree of aggressive behaviour. There is a reason why there is such a strong connection between our children's violent behaviour and violent TV.

I wonder if even the older children know any more what is real and what is fantasy. A teen mob attacked a sixteen year old boy outside a suburban church in Victoria.[27] There were fifty teens there to witness a revenge fight. The victim was just in the wrong place at the wrong time, because the mob was looking for a different teen. Some of the young people were there just to witness the fight, and some of them were there to record it on video cameras. One of them is reported as saying "You better hurry up and make this happen. I'm running out of film."

At the end of the discussion of media and violence Wallin said, "It seems like a chicken and egg problem. At what point is it possible to break the escalating cycle of more and more angry confrontation and violence?"

Escalating Cycles

To date people have said that they want less anger and violence, but, in fact, the attempts to stop the anger and violence in our society have been minimal. For example, there have been numerous suggestions as to how to respond to violence in the media, but precious little action. In Canada the only response has been a Voluntary Code Regarding Violence on Television Programming implemented in Canada in 1994. This was used to take Mighty Morphin Power Rangers off Canadian TV. However, taking one violent children's program off TV has done little. The latest response has been the new technological development of the V-Chip. The assumption has been, and continues to be, that parents through a V-Chip or just turning off the TV can monitor and protect their children from the TV violence. Pulitzer Prize winning journalist and mother Ellen Goodman has said that mothers and fathers are expected to screen virtually every aspect of their children's lives. Parents become a kind of "alternative culture" struggling to have their values prevail.

It is interesting to consider the value of anger in the mainstream, or in an alternative culture. Do parents, like most people in our culture, consider anger a good thing? For many people anger is seen as a tool to control and punish. This theory is linked to the carrot and stick school of psychology, known as Behaviourism. Anger is used to punish the wrongdoer. If the wrongdoers are really bad, then the anger escalates into violence and finally death. It is all a part of the belief that punishment will teach them a lesson. A cartoon that illustrates this is of a man hitting a child, and saying "This will teach you to hit your brother."

Our whole society is caught up in the belief in anger and revenge, usually called punishment, as a means of controlling bad people. It is not only the people in California who believe in three-strikes-and-you-are-out. To my amazement I read an article in the Globe and Mail where a mother explained how her seven year old child's school policy was three-strikes-and-you-are-out.[28] Her son squirted juice in the lunch room, yelled in a loud voice and had a magnifying glass on the lunch room table. She was informed that he was suspended for one week. When she objected, the principal and vice-principal explained that they had to keep control of the lunch room.

Not only do we believe that anger will control other people, we think that anger will motivate us to do something about the bad people and the unjust world. Whenever I have talked to people about anger, the first response is that it is a good thing. However, if we keep talking a script is laid out. There is a bad thing, an unjust situation or a bad person doing something wrong. Then there is anger, and then finally a response. I usually ask "Why does the anger have to be part of the script?" There is usually silence, and no answer.

Anger is not a motivator, rather it is part of a cycle of negative feelings. Many people, even those who say anger is good, will acknowledge that anger is linked to the other three negative feelings: fear, blame and despair. In parenting courses, such as Parent Effectiveness Training, there is a recognition that there is a connection between anger and the other emotions. June Crawford and her colleagues talk about how anger and depression frequently co-exist. Carol Saussy talks about how anger can be confused with fear, and how it clusters with other emotions.[29] Given the recognition by countless experts that anger is linked to the other negative emotions, it is amazing that there is an overwhelming belief that anger can be lifted out of the negative cycle and used as a motivator.

Justice-Seekers

One of my favourite discussions on this topic was with Sara, my young social activist friend. I said, "Sara, what do you think of anger?" "Anger is a motivating force," said Sara. Then I asked her if anger motivated her. "Oh, no," she said, "Anger doesn't motivate me." "What does?" I asked. "Oh, I have an innate sense of justice," she said.

Justice-seekers need power, and in order to have power I need to change my script. I need to change my role so that I am no longer a powerless victim. How do we stop feeling powerless? My husband and I struggled for years over this question as we did our best to raise our children, and to help other parents raise their children. We finally concluded that to be empowered one needs to make sense of the world, to feel good about oneself and others, to have alternatives to choose from, and to be able to act. There is no need to feel angry in order to have power.

It is a paradox that those who feel most powerless are those who try the hardest to control others and the world. This is clearest in families where there is abuse. Abuse of any kind is used in an effort to control the other person. The reason why the abuser feels the need to strike out is that he or she feels powerless. The more powerless we feel, the angrier we are. The abuser feels like he or she is a powerless victim, because outside causes "make him angry." A classic case is one where a husband who hits his wife states "She made me angry." He believes that. We are all taught to believe that, and we all end up feeling powerless.

Not only do I have the ability to change my role as helpless victim, I have the ability to change the role of the people around me. I have discovered that it is possible to change one's perception of the people around us from evil demons to people. They may be misguided, or hopelessly wrong in their perceptions of how the world works, and I might totally disagree with them. However, my anger will make any kind of dialogue impossible. After my meeting with the other social activists I sought out my friend whom I had snapped at. I apologized for my inappropriate anger. She was gracious enough to say "I understand. You probably had a bad day." I agreed, and said that I was glad that she was able to put aside my harsh words. We could continue to work side by side on issues that matter to us both.

When the angry words between myself and my friend occurred she responded in the same way as my politician classmate did. Both responded to anger with anger. In both these cases the angry response was a temporary one. Neither my friend, nor I, wanted to stay angry. In the case of the MLA I recognized my anger and said "Let's agree to disagree." Then she also cooled down, and in order to show me that she really was a caring person she asked me about my qualifications. She said that she wanted to help me find work, and she said that she would get back to me. She adopted the "helper" role. I never heard from her again, and I did not expect to. It was only her way of showing that she was not really a bad person.

Finally, I acknowledge that the world is full of pain and suffering. I have struggled with how to deal with that. The question of suffering is one that people have grappled with since the dawn of time. I can only look at so much pain. I do not get involved with Amnesty International because, for me, the pain is too great.

I look at the National Film Board video and I see the suffering of my fellow Canadians. And if that was all there was I would be swallowed up in powerless rage. But I know that the world is filled with beauty and with beautiful people struggling together. And I have another video to look at. It is called "We are the People. Listen to Us." It was put together by a group of non-employed Canadians. We had a conference, and we taped it and made a video. At the end of the conference we stood in a circle, and held hands and sang. And that is power and hope. For me there is no longer any place for anger. There is only joy in the power of the people.

SECTION II
WELFARE,
WORKFARE, WORK
CAMPS, WHAT NEXT?

*Does anyone ask what we are going to do with all the people
we first throw out of work and then throw off welfare?*
MICHAEL VALPY, GLOBE AND MAIL, JULY 19,1996

*How did things get this bad? This is a question virtually
every progressive Canadian has asked themselves in recent
months and years.*
MURRAY DOBBIN,
The New Right and How Things Got This Bad

I WAS SITTING IN THE FRONT ROW AT A FORUM organized by Winnipeg Harvest food bank. A number of politicians were talking about poverty and what should be done about it. The Deputy Mayor of Winnipeg was explaining the world as he saw it, and he punctuated every second sentence with "The reality is . . ." I did not believe in his reality and after a while whenever he said "The reality is . . ." I would say in a loud voice "No, it isn't." At first he carried on but then he began to punctuate every second sentence with "Well, I believe that . . ."

The Deputy Mayor, the Mayor, the Premier, the Finance Minister, the Prime Minister all believe that they know what reality is. Each person has in his or her head a model of how the world works and this model is based on certain values. The model and the values lead the person to make certain decisions and to act in certain ways.

People will hold on to their reality in the face of all kinds of troubling questions. Facts will be pushed around, ignored, slightly altered or embellished so that everything neatly fits. But the problem is that today there are too many troublesome facts and too many people that do not fit. As Michael Valpy says "What are we going to do with all these people?"

Welfare does not seem to be the answer. Therefore all our governments, both federal and provincial, keep cutting welfare rates to lower and lower levels in the hope that people will go and get a job. This does not seem to work either. So the governments decide to give them a job at less than minimum wage, with no health and safety standards and no right to form a union (Workfare). The people still do not get out there and get a real job. So finally the governments have taken away the right to welfare, and have begun to deny welfare to people. First the undeserving, those with addictions, then those who fail to keep appointments.

At first glance our leaders' present course may seem heartless and cruel. At times, I am tempted to think of them as evil men and women. But in terms of their reality both cutting welfare and cutting jobs are logical actions to take. Their actions are logical because they believe that, in the long run, everyone will benefit. At a meeting of the House of Commons Standing Committee on Finance held in Winnipeg in December 1995, David Walker, then Liberal MP for Winnipeg North Centre, told me that the government's present course of action would benefit his children.

We will look at the present course of action in Canada today in the following four chapters. Then maybe we can decide if this course of action will benefit David Walker's children, or my children, or Canada's children, or anybody's children.

CHAPTER 5
THE MONOPOLY GAME
or VACUUM CLEANER
ECONOMICS

The mantra of the moment is still trickle-down economics. The rich are encouraged to earn as much as they like in the hope that the poor will be better off because the crumbs will be larger. In practice it hasn't worked that way.
VICTOR KEEGAN, GLOBE AND MAIL, AUG.10,1996

The poor have occasionally rebelled against being governed badly. The rich have always rebelled against being governed at all.
G.K. CHESTERTON, *What's Wrong with the World?*

ONE OF MY FAVOURITE GAMES as a child was Monopoly. Has anyone not spent hours around a table in the pursuit of Boardwalk and Park Place? And just as you near the elusive property you need in order to make a set, you land in jail. You moan. The others laugh and cheer. The game continues. Finally there is one winner with all the money and all the property. The game is over and put away for another day. Life, real life, continues and no one is hurt. Everyone has a chance to win tomorrow.

It was in 1993, at the Church and Community Inquiry into Unemployment, that it first dawned on me that the game Monopoly is based on the economic system that we live in. I decided to make a presentation to the seven panel members who were looking at the issue of unemployment. The question in my mind was "How do you challenge the common wisdom of the society? How do you make it possible for people to look at things from a different angle, in a new light?" For most people, the idea of challenging the basic economic theory of our society would not be common sense. It would be nonsense. So I thought that rather than challenge the economic theory, I would challenge the idea of having a society based on the Monopoly game. This caused a little stir at the time. Francis Russell, a Winnipeg Free Press columnist, wrote the idea up in her column. Then the idea, and the whole Inquiry, and its report, was filed.

The idea of living in a Monopoly game still intrigues me. The Monopoly game is fairly simple. It is based on supply and demand, and private ownership, the two key elements of Free Enterprise or Capitalism. Real life, however, isn't as simple. Real economic life includes things like government, labour, and technological change. How do these fit into the game? In order to understand how all the elements fit together I was forced to look at economics.

It has taken me a long time to figure out, to understand and then explain what is happening. I have never taken an economics course. My daughter has a degree in Economics and I have looked at her textbooks. They are incomprehensible to me. I am reminded of my daughters' friend Sara. She was working on a newsletter with my daughters that had to be done and to be at the printer the next day. At two in the morning she was hunched over her computer with her head in her hands saying "head hurts, head hurts." That is how I feel when I look at the Economics textbooks. But I think I have figured out the basics. So if I can figure it out, it is possible for anyone.

Lets start with the word "economics." The word comes

from the Greek "eco" which means "household." The study of how the economy works or "economics" is the study of running the household. When I was at the University of Manitoba in the 1960s there was the Faculty of Home Economics and the Department of Political Economy. Now both department names are changed. We have the Faculty of Human Ecology, instead of the Faculty of Home Economics. We have the Department of Economics instead of the Department of Political Economy. Because the adjective "political" has been dropped, we forget that people originally assumed the public, or politics was involved. I find it helpful if I remember what economics originally meant, and what I think it still means. <u>Economics is the study of how we run the public household.</u>

I went to the dictionary for a definition and discovered that "economics" is "the science of the production, distribution and consumption of goods and services." This is interesting. First it says that "economics is a science." By that it implies that economics is objective and value free, just like one plus one is two, or combining one atom of oxygen and two atoms of hydrogen will produce H_2O or water. If this were the case then all economists would agree on the basics. Chemists are agreed that H_2O is water. However, I have listened many times to economists disagreeing about everything. I remember being one of the speakers at St. Paul's College at their seventh Annual Paulinian Conference. One of the panels had two economists from the University of Manitoba discussing poverty and unemployment. They disagreed on everything. So I don't really think we can agree with the dictionary that economics is a science.

Next the dictionary says that economics deals with the production, distribution and consumption of goods and services. This is true. This definition is talking about the market. However, the other two main components of economics have been left out. In any household there is the question of who owns what and who makes the rules. In our public household there is the question of ownership (who owns what) and government (who makes the rules).

The dictionary looks only at markets, and Monopoly looks only at markets and ownership. Why is this? I think it must have happened because of how economic theory developed over the years.

For most of history people have bee chugging along providing for themselves and their families. People have been producing, distributing and consuming food and clothes and shelter. But eventually, as was bound to happen, someone decided to put together a theory about how this game was played, or rather how the game should be played.

Along came Adam Smith and *The Wealth of Nations* in 1776, and modern economics began. Adam Smith developed and expanded laissez-faire economics or leave-it-alone economics. He said that if you leave the market alone and don't interfere, then 'an invisible hand' will ensure that the greatest good for the greatest number will inevitably happen. Thus from the very beginning of modern economics the theory (and remember, it is just a theory) was that government should only be involved minimally in the economy.

It was inevitable that someone should come along and challenge the theory. After all the "invisible hand" didn't seem to be doing a very good job for millions and millions of people. In the nineteenth century a man by the name of Karl Marx suggested another theory. Then came others who said that Marxism was too extreme, but the government should be involved. There is democratic socialism, and social democracy, and lots of theories about how much the government should be involved in the public household. When the government gets involved it sets rules for the game. The issue is: what rules, and how many rules and who makes the rules. We will put these issues of government involvement into Chapter Seven.

For now, let's look at the two main components of Monopoly, or Free Enterprise, or Capitalism. They are markets and ownership.

MARKETS

"To market to market to buy a fat pig.
Home again, home again, jiggety jig."
"This little piggy went to market.
This little piggy stayed home."

We hear about the market place before we can walk or talk. Buying and selling goods and services using money happens all around us. The toddler in the store cries "Buy me this, mommy."

There was a time when most Canadians lived on farms and were more or less self-sufficient for their daily food. But the farmer needed to sell his crop in order to prosper. Today there is no longer, indeed, there never was, the completely self-sufficient person or family. We all live in a money economy. We are all part of the market. We all buy and sell. There are four things that people buy and sell.

1) Labour Market

For most of us, the average Canadian, there are only two markets we worry about. First and foremost is the labour market. Can we sell our labour in order to get money? If we can't we are "up shit creek without a paddle." If we can't get money we can't buy goods or services. We can't buy food, or clothes, or shelter, or bus tickets, or a cup of coffee.

The people that run this country have not noticed that

the current information technology revolution is as extensive and radical as the Industrial Revolution. The technological changes of the Industrial Revolution meant that people left the farms, went to the cities, and worked in the factories. People could sell their labour. The conditions were appalling at first. Gradually they improved thanks to the union movement. People were given more and more money. People were able to buy what they needed.

Today the labour of men and women is needed less and less. More and more of us are shut out of the labour market. We are no longer in the game!

2) Consumer Market

For those still in the game, those with money, there is an ongoing interest in how much things cost. Here is where we encounter the traditional economic theory of supply and demand. When I told my friend Shelly that I was writing a chapter on economics, she said "All I know about economics is supply and demand." She did not mean that she knew what supply and demand meant. She knew the words. That is all that most of us

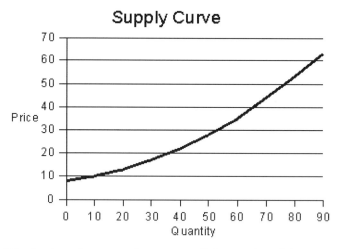

The higher the price the more will be produced by companies.

who are not involved in business know - the words. We need to understand the basic supply and demand theory, because it is often trotted out to show how important it is for governments to stay out of the market.

Here I will draw my one and only series of graphs.

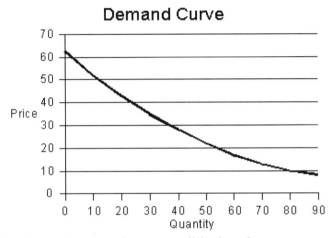

The lower the price the more will be bought.

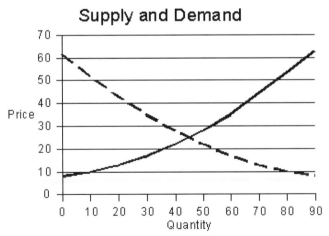

In a "free market" the price will tend towards the "equilibrium" point where the two curves cross.

We are told that this supply and demand curve which considers only two variables is so important that nothing should disturb it. Here is the "free market." Because it is called "free" it seems like a good thing. How can anyone be against freedom? The problem with "free market" freedom is that it is not connected to anything. It is only rights, no responsibilities.

3) Stock Market

The consumer market has been around for thousands of years, but the stock market is a fairly recent invention. It is the defining part of modern capitalism. Capitalism, as we know it, began in the seventeenth century. Corporations were recognised as persons. Therefore, they had the right to enter into contracts. The people who set up these corporations were allowed to set up limited liability corporations. Notice that at the end of a corporate name you see "Ltd." This means that if you buy stock in a company, your responsibility is limited to the amount of money you put in. When Consumers Distributing went bankrupt, the people who owned the stock in Consumers were not responsible for the whole debt. Thus, other companies that were owed money by Consumers also went bankrupt. Consumers owed Jolly Jumper $500,000 dollars, so Jolly Jumper also went bankrupt. No one was responsible.

Now it's true that the stock market also is part of the "free market" and is concerned only with supply and demand. However, there is a big difference between the stock market and the consumer market. The consumer market deals with goods and services. I thought that the stock market also dealt with things like shoes (goods) and restaurants (services). I soon discovered that, in fact, only 5% of the transactions in the stock exchange deal with actual goods and services. The other 95% deals with things like futures, derivatives, and other abstract entities that have nothing to do with the every day lives of ordinary people. There is a whole world out there where trillions of dollars are exchanged every day and only 5% of the transactions are connected to goods and services.[30]

For those of you interested in the meaning of these weird things like futures and derivatives, purchasing futures is when you pay now for shares you will collect at some pre-determined future date. When purchasing derivatives, instead of bidding on the future price of a commodity, you bet on the future price of a price. These things do not always work. Remember the guy in the red suspenders that brought down Britain's Baring Bank? This was done by gambling on derivatives.

4) Money Market

Finally we come to the money market. The other morning, I woke up and turned on CBC Radio. I heard the interviewer ask someone how the money market was doing. There was a long discussion around exchange rates, that is, how much the Canadian dollar is worth. They discussed how if the worth of the dollar went up, this was good for people who wanted to holiday in Florida. It was also good for people that import goods. On the other hand, if the Canadian dollar went down, then this was good for people who wanted to export things. A low Canadian dollar increases the number of tourists who want to come to Canada, because their money is worth more here.

Dare I confess that the first time I wrote this I got it backwards. My daughter, who was typing it, said "Mom, I think if the Canadian dollar goes down it is good for exports, not imports." At this point I nearly despaired! But I kept going. I have to and so do you. If we don't we will never understand why and how we are being made paupers in one of the richest countries in the world.

The radio discussion ended. The key question, of course, was never asked. Who decides if the Canadian dollar goes up or down? I had always assumed that governments had a say in this important decision. The next day the "Ten Days for Global Justice" kit arrived. An article in the kit explained that in the early 1970s capitalist countries decided to let their currency "float." They gave up the link between money and precious metals. The currency of a country became just another commodity to buy and sell. It is indeed a "free market." Brokers and bankers and other free market players, most of whom are invisible, make the decisions about our dollar. Whether it goes up or down depends on who can make the most money from whom.

OWNERSHIP

What is the purpose, the goal, of all this buying and selling? The goal is the same as the goal in Monopoly. In Monopoly you are in the game to win it all, to own it all.

1) Owning and growing money

This obsession with owning money is everywhere. There is Harold Geneen, the former CEO of the multinational conglomerate ITT, whose goal was "ten percent growth in earnings per share per year." There is my elderly relative who says she loves going to the bank and getting her bankbook up to date, because she can "see her money grow." Harold Geneen really worked at getting more. My relative lets the bank do her work for her.

How does money grow? We all know about interest, but I'm not sure that we all know about compound interest. Compound interest means that you get interest on the interest. I never really understood how powerful compound interest was until August 16, 1995. I read an article in the Winnipeg Free Press. The article told us how a refugee centre got a $94,000 dollar cheque from the City because it won a tax appeal. Great, I thought. How wonderful for them. I continued to read the article and discovered that the refund they were entitled to was $52,000 dollars. However, because there was a three year delay before this was settled, they received another $42,000 dollars, which was compound interest on the refund. This was a good thing for the refugee centre. They paid off their deficit. But what is this incredible mechanism - compound interest - doing to the society we live in?

2) Owning the means of production

When modern capitalism began, the issue of ownership of land, factories, and equipment was so important that it formed the base of a whole new theory - Marxism. Karl Marx saw that the rich were getting richer and the poor were starving. The rich were getting richer because they owned the means of production. Marx believed that those who did the work should reap the benefits. So he proposed that the workers, or the community as a whole, should own the means of production. This was revolutionary. He was proposing a revolution. The life of peasants in feudal societies, like Russia and China, were so hard, and they had so little that the people looked to Marxism. Communist revolutions were seen to be the only solution to utter destitution.

In the Western world, the powers that be were smart enough to know that something had to be done for the workers, or we too would have a revolution. I remember watching a television program on US President Franklin Delano Roosevelt. It was the Dirty Thirties and there were many people in the United States who thought the only way to get justice was to have a communist revolution. But F.D.R. brought in so many benefits for workers in his New Deal, that the impetus for a revolution was greatly diminished.

Here in Canada we had people like J.S. Woodsworth, who lead the Co-operative Commonwealth Federation. The CCF was composed of people from a variety of groups. Farmers, workers and intellectuals gathered together in Regina in 1933; the Regina Manifesto was written; and the CCF was born. In the document there was a plan to nationalize major segments of the Canadian economy. Banks, in particular, were earmarked for nationalization. The call for nationalizing our natural resource industries and banks was a means to make life better for ordinary Canadians.

Before the CCF was created Woodsworth and A.A. Heaps were elected as the Independent Labour Party. They pushed the Liberal government to bring in Old Age Pensions and relief for the unemployed. This was finally achieved by an agreement between Woodsworth and Prime Minister McKenzie King. Woodsworth agreed to support the 1926 minority Liberal government, if they would bring in these radical new social programs. This was the beginning of Canada's Social Security System.

Step by step the lives of ordinary Canadians were changed for the better. The CCF, and its successor the NDP, pushed for more and more social programs, the most significant for many being Medicare. There was less and less talk about owning the means of production. Canada developed a society balanced between free market capitalism and socialism.

3) Owning one's country

Things might have carried on in this way for many more years. However, with the invention of the microchip the global capital market intensified. We have now moved from the Industrial Revolution to the Cybernetic Revolution. Computers mean that buying and selling can be done in cyberspace. Money can be made without actual people or production of goods and services. Big money can be made by guessing if a currency will go up or down by one-onehundredth of a percentage point.

The supply and demand market place used to mean supply and demand of labour, goods and services, stock, and money within a certain country. However, the underlying assumption of the market place that "bigger is better" meant that as soon as business was able to jump over borders then the "bigger" meant the whole wide world, or globalization.

Borders, or boundaries have no meaning for capitalism. The game has now expanded. For those in the Monopoly game, the issue of owning one's country has no relevance. Capitalism is only concerned with nation states as enforcers of corporate rule. For those of us outside the game, the issue of owning our country is now the most important issue of all.

Most Canadians are still asleep on this issue. There are many who have been trying to wake us up. The most obvious is the Council of Canadians, who since the 1988 election have been striving mightily to explain the issue to Canadians. I recently saw a quote attributed to Eric Kierans in "The World We Want" which seems to sum it all up.

"What is a borderless world? It is a world emptied of every value and principle - except one, accumulation"

The goal of Monopoly, accumulating wealth, seems to be picking up speed. The 354 billionaires in the world now have more wealth than the bottom three billion people on this planet.

The people running the game still have most of us believing that the crumbs will trickle down. But more and more of us now understand that whatever crumbs there may be are being quickly vacuumed up.

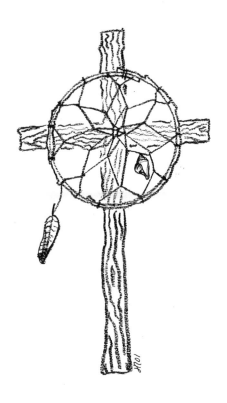

CHAPTER 6
THE GODS WE WORSHIP

Unless I am much mistaken the Golden Rule is still the same: invest where the profits are highest, quickest and safest. If that means crushing a few, or many, or numerous human beings, it is regrettable, but the reasoning goes, that it is the inevitable price of progress.

ARCHBISHOP HELDER CAMARO, *The Dorothy Day Book*

The state ideological system can be compared to religion, in that it is not subjected to scientific or objective analysis and is put forward to be accepted on faith . . . the nature of the capitalist ideology - the glorification of competition, individualism, greed and the pursuit of power and wealth.

HOWARD ADAMS, *A Tortured People: The Politics of Colonization*

O NE SUNDAY MORNING as I flipped on the television I heard a man called Stuart Briscoe say that every individual worships something. The only question is who or what. If we have no gods we make them up. I do not think we make up new gods. I have a feeling that all the gods have been there from the beginning. What we make up are the names to identify them. Some of the old names remain in our memory and do not change. We still recognize that the worship of Mammon is the worship of money. We have probably forgotten that the worship of Baal is really the worship of the tribal gods. The tribal gods are still with us under many different names. Tribal, ethnic and religious fanaticism is alive and well all over the world.

In Canada for many years most people worshiped the Christian God. The mainline churches varied in ritual, form and doctrine, but there was little fanaticism. In fact, in the prairies there was an amazing accommodation as churches politely divided up the prairies between them. Now for most people in Canadian society the traditional Christian God has receded further and further away from their lives. Formal worship of God in mainstream churches declines every year. The pews are filled with gray heads. The churches lose their membership and their influence. The society, as a whole, no longer even remembers what God is worshiped in the buildings. When my daughter was in Grade One, twenty years ago, she was the only child in her class who knew what Easter was really about.

The need to worship is fundamental to human beings. The decline in formal worship comes about as we become less and less human beings and more and more machines. In industry and business people are looked upon as identical replaceable parts. What happens to those parts is no longer the concern of business or government. Both will "downsize" and take no responsibility for the people who have lost their livelihood. The people that lose their jobs are not the brothers and sisters of those making the decisions. They are called a "human resource." A human resource is considered much like any other resource, much like any other machine. Thus if we are truly only individual machines, then talking about gods and worshiping them is indeed nonsense.

I do not believe that people are machines. I believe that we love and value different things and that this is the root of all our problems. The Bible says "the love of money is the root of all evil." What we love is what we worship. We need to name the gods we unconsciously love. For unless we identify the gods that we worship, the things that we most value, then nothing makes sense, and nothing will change.

Not only has it been unacceptable to talk about our gods, the chief object of our love, it has been considered unacceptable to talk about values. But a change is beginning to happen. People are beginning to write about values. One of the best writers in the field of world hunger and Third World issues is Frances Moore Lappe. For twenty years she wrote books on the causes of and solutions to poverty and world hunger. Then there was a change. In 1989 she wrote a book called *Rediscovering America's Values*. After twenty years she came to the conclusion that all her work was not changing anything. She had all the facts and statistics and suggestions for doing things differently, but nothing was changing. She realized that before people can change their actions, their values have to change.

I have only discovered a few others who have focused on the value base of society. One such group is "Ten Days for Global Justice." This is a cooperative venture of Anglican, Evangelical Lutheran, Presbyterian, and United churches and the Canadian Catholic Organization for Development and Peace. Twenty years ago I was on the National Committee for this organization and as I remember it the focus was all on the same things that Frances Moore Lappe was writing about. The main theme for years was "Give a man a fish and feed him for one day. Teach a man to fish and feed him for life." The slogan represented a change of perspective from charity to justice. The focus was on broader issues such as why people were hungry and what kinds of things could be done to bring about change in the society. At that time values were not a prominent part of the discussion. However, the underlying presumption was that we knew what our values were and that we all had the same values.

It was with great interest that I began to read the 1997

Education and Action guide for "Ten Days for Global Justice." The introduction to the theme "The World We Want" tells us that last year's theme was "There are Alternatives." This year the focus was on the values that form the foundation of our alternatives. From the article it was clear that deciding on this approach had been a struggle. Would the writers be considered too idealistic? Would talking about values seem unconnected to concrete alternatives? Imagine. Even church organizations feel uncomfortable talking about values. It is as if everyone, including those involved with religion, have decided to ignore the most powerful aspect of people's lives.

In our culture there was no conscious decision, made by the majority of citizens, to ignore values. Rather, values were just quietly dropped out of the discussion. This was the logical outcome of adopting a particular understanding of what is real. The media, politicians and other "experts" are obsessed by the quest for reality. It is only in the last few years that I have been conscious of a continual refrain of "The reality is . . ." and "The facts are . . ." However, only certain aspects of reality are a part of this refrain. Only things that are concrete, measurable, scientific are considered real. Only the measurable parts of people are considered real. We measure our biological components and know that we have a certain blood type. Emotions and values are not measurable. Therefore, emotions and values do not exist.

Every aspect of our lives is now discussed without any mention of values. This was brought home to me a few years ago. We went to my son's school to learn about the new family life education course that was to be introduced in the school. The teacher explained everything, including the sex-education component. We were then encouraged to ask questions. I said that the focus was entirely on the mechanics of sexual intercourse. How did it address issues such as the relationship between men and women and when it was appropriate to engage in sexual activity? The teacher replied that no such subjects were discussed. "Teachings on sex-education are value-free."

There is, I admit, one phrase that is still used by some politicians that implies that values are still part of the discussion. It is the phrase "family values." The phrase is usually spoken by those whose policies are destroying Canadian families. The term is thrown into conversation as though everyone knew exactly what it meant. I have never heard any politician explain what he or she meant by "family values." I have never heard any reporter ask anyone what they mean by the phrase. I suspect what is meant by "family values" is that "Me and my family come first."

I, too, believe in "family values." The difference is that I believe that the community, the society, should be run like a family, where the strong protect the weak, not push them over the cliff. My "family values" are actually in direct opposition to the values that are held by most of our leaders. The values that underline most of the decisions taken by government and business in our country are usually known as "market values."

The "market values" and all the other values so highly prized by our leaders are seldom challenged. We had one great philosopher in Canada who challenged not only the market values, but also the technological value of faster, more efficient, unlimited growth, and unlimited individual freedom. George Grant, in *Lament for a Nation*, his many other writings, and his radio broadcasts on the CBC called these values into question. They were becoming our priority values, our gods.

George Grant was writing from the 1950s to the 1980s. He called us to remember other values that had shaped Canadian life. Our social programs, from Old Age Pensions to Unemployment Insurance to Medicare, were based on the value of the common good and our responsibility for each other and for our community. Now market values have overtaken family values. The result is what Rick Salutin called "a happy logo culture."[31] He was talking about our premiers, who were wearing vests that said Canadian Airlines at their conference. The Canadian Taxpayers Federation thought this was a good idea because it saved us money. Rick Salutin felt that elected leaders should not be a walking logo for an airline. He felt that the "happy logo culture" was a totally different culture from traditional Canadian culture.

Several months later Salutin decided that we have gone further than the "happy logo culture." He wrote that we are past logos and on to monuments. No longer do we build cathedrals. Now we build huge monuments with company logos on them. These are meant to be permanent, and to show the power of "the Great God Business."[32]

MAMMON

The only game in town is now the Monopoly game. The highest compliment you can pay any enterprise is that it is run like a business. We are told that our governments should be run like a business. In order to achieve this, more and more of the public sector is either totally sold to business, i.e. privatized, or business infiltrates it bit by bit, as in schools and prisons. Whether sports or the arts, whether education or government, everything is measured by "the bottom line." The bottom line is the line at the bottom of a profit and loss statement that tells us how much money was made, what the profit was.

If all of society is to be run like a business, then where do the profits of the business go? The profits go either to the corporation and its stockholders or to senior management. We all know the banks make billions of dollars a year. Now we are learning how much the CEOs of banks and corporations make in a year. The 1995 poster put out by the Jesuit Centre for Social Faith and Justice details how much CEOs make in a year. They were paid on average over $2.6 million dollars in 1995, nearly ninety times the average wage of working Canadians. There is no limit to how much either an individual or a corporation can accumulate.

We used to call the lust for more and more money greed. A few people are willing to name the excessive accumulation and worship of money as greed. There was a television program on CBC on the Bre-X incident. At that time three billion dollars worth of Bre-X market capitalization had disappeared as the stock plummeted. The interviewer asked the market analyst Douglas Leishmen what he attributed this disaster to. His answer was "market madness and human greed." [33]

GLOBAL GROWTH

In order to accumulate more and more money one has to believe in growth. In capitalism there is a mechanism whereby money grows exponentially. It is called compound interest. There is also a guideline religiously followed. It is the principle of 10% growth in earnings per share. There is no limit to this growth. In order for this unlimited growth to continue, the next logical step was for national corporations to become multi-national or trans-national corporations.

Globalization not only means global corporations. It also means that nations are told what to do by the international regulatory bodies called the World Bank and the International Monetary Fund. These organizations were established in 1944 at the Bretton Woods conference. By the 1990s their policy was focusing on global competitiveness and debt/deficit reduction.

They implemented Structural Adjustment Programs in the Third World. This meant that in order to get loans from the World Bank, Third World countries had to privatize their government programs and cut back their government services. These policies are all implemented because of the total commitment to business and profit. Poulose Mar Poulose of India tells us that "the market economy has become a cult and the places that they worship are at the World Bank and the IMF."

Finally globalization means that we no longer have national boundaries. Not only do corporations grow, they push the governments of sovereign nations to make treaties that break down national boundaries. James Laxer has written a book called *False God: How the Globalization Myth has Impoverished Canada*. Laxer talks about how the state is seen as a barrier to efficiency that must be broken down. Ultimately, we will no longer be citizens, only consumers.

The trade agreements around the world mean that countries no longer can make decisions concerning their own citizens without the permission of other countries. For example, the Free Trade Agreement guarantees US corporations "national treatment" in Canada. This means that a US company can claim compensation from any Canadian government, provincial or federal, if it decides to take a sector of the economy into public ownership. Many people believe that this is the reason why Bob Rae's NDP government in Ontario did not follow through on its election promise to bring a public auto insurance system to Ontario.

Where does globalization end? Just as there is no end to the amount of money a corporation or a person may own, there is now no limit to globalization. The old rules governing world trade were outlined in the GATT (General Agreement on Tariffs and Trade). I always remembered the name of this organization because there was an ecumenical group called GATT-FLY that used to report on its activities. Now we have the World Trade Organization (WTO). This new organization is busily setting up new rules governing world trade. Bill Blaikie, the NDP M.P. for Winnipeg-Transcona, says that the GATT was concerned with reducing tariff barriers and the WTO is concerned with eliminating them. Blaikie calls this a sea change in international governance that threatens democracy.

Francis Russell says "the state withers away." She explains how the WTO plans to carry out its objectives. The industrialized countries are getting ready to sign a Multilateral Investment Agreement. "The MAI (Multi-lateral Agreement on Investment) will mean most of the important law-making and policy setting powers exercised by sovereign states will be ceded to multi-national corporations. The "National Treatment" section of the Canada-US Free Trade Agreement will be expanded to include the world. The MAI meant corporations would decide employment policy, taxation policy, labour policy, social policy and investment policy. What will be left for democratically elected governments to decide?"[34]

The growth of capital and corporations can be thought of like the growth of a cancer. Just as a cancer in one's body is a cell that grows continually and with nothing to stop it, globalization continues. When I think about a cancerous growth it is scary. I actually prefer to think of something that has grown too big, as people who wrote fairy stories think of the overgrown. They are called giants, and they are stupid, and we can defeat them. We defeated the MAI.

But for now the elites of our society continue to worship growth. The Globe and Mail editorial heading is "The next mantra should be growth."[35] In Bill Blaikie's article concerning the WTO summit in Singapore he says "If there is a unifying vision among the governments of the world, it is trade liberalization. Everyone had to repeat the same mantra, pay homage to the same god."

HARD WORK

In order to accumulate more and more money one has to work hard. It is interesting that those who are born with money seem to also work hard in order to gain more. Everyone, whether rich or poor, seems to be under this moral obligation to keep working harder and harder in order to gain more and more money. Thus it becomes clear that the main god is Mammon, wealth.

The justification for the hard work is what used to be called the "Protestant Work Ethic." It is the height of irony that the idol of hard work is labeled the "Protestant Work Ethic." This happened because a man called Max Weber wrote a book called *The Protestant Ethic and the Spirit of Capitalism* in 1958. He used Protestantism, specifically Calvinism, to justify the Capitalist economic system. He pointed out that the mercantile economy emerged at the same time as Protestantism. Since both emerged around the same time, the argument goes that one caused the other.

The obvious fact that Weber and thousands of others have failed to grasp is that the Protestant reformation's core idea was that people are justified with God through faith, not by works. We are not good people and loved by God because we work hard. Rather, we are in a right relationship with a loving God through faith.

We no longer talk about the "Protestant Work Ethic." We have lost the knowledge of the origin of the term. However, the "work ethic" continues to be held up as the justification of one's life. The main-stream media continue to reinforce the worship of hard work. One of the columnists in the Winnipeg Sun writes about stay-at-home parents who do not have paid work. The headline reads "Stay-at-home parents plan ignores work ethic." She refers to the poor immigrant Winnipeg families that taught their kids that you work for what you want. This theory was also pointed out to me by the minister I previously quoted in Chapter Two. He talked about his immigrant parents and how hard they worked. Do people really believe that the working farmers of previous generations are an example for working people today who have been laid off or fired? Can we really offer these people free homesteads if they work the land? What exactly are they supposed to work at if there is no paid work?

For some strange reason people who do not have paid work are pictured as "sitting at home living off the rest of us," as the columnist wrote, or, as our Prime Minister stated "sitting at home drinking beer and watching TV." The unpaid work that is done for the good of the household or the community goes on every day. Every household and every family requires time-consuming hard work. The work that is done caring for the household economy is, according to Marilyn Waring "the single largest productive and service sector in the Canadian economy." She points to the statistical data done in Australia in national time-use surveys. The household economy in Australia is worth $348 billion dollars on an annual basis. The market economy is worth $362 billion dollars. There is a small gap of 4% between the two. But only market economy workers are considered "real" workers.

It is not only our political leaders and media columnists who fear that people are not working hard enough. In the 1974 Federal Work Ethic and Job Satisfaction survey, it was found that people believe that the work ethic is declining for others, but that they are hard workers. People said that they wanted to work, but that our social institutions made it easy for others to avoid working. Thus, everyone seems to be working hard, but believes their fellow citizens are not. Our leaders continually reinforce this analysis, so that only those fortunate enough to have work in the market economy will be considered valuable citizens. The rest of us are labelled the "undeserving lazy poor."

The very phrase "undeserving poor" refers to people living in poverty who, it is judged , do not work hard. Officially we call this group of people the "employable" poor. Any group of people can be put into this category with the stoke of a pen. One minute a group of people are labeled "non-employable" i.e. not expected to work in the market economy. The next minute the same group of people are labeled "employable." Now they are the "undeserving poor." This is what happened in Manitoba in 1996. Mothers with children over six years of age went from being "non-employable" to "employable" by government decree. Thus we now have thousands more people who are considered the "undeserving poor." This group of people are expected to get into the market economy or starve.

EDUCATION AND TRAINING

How does one enter the market economy? The answer for years had been education. Now the answer is training.

Once education was for the upper classes. Training was for the lower classes, those workers who lacked the ability or the means for a higher education. Then education became available for the vast working middle class of Canadians. Thousands of us went to university. We gained what was once called a liberal arts education. When I went to university I took a BA first. I did not even have a major subject. I took English and History and Philosophy and Religion. I was involved in a wide range of student activities. I went to a conference put on by the Student Christian Movement. People were discussing Bonhoeffer and Niebuhr and Tillich and Harvey Cox's *The Secular City*. The world opened up for me. I became an educated person.

Now education has once more become only available for those who have money. The rest of us are told we need training for jobs in the new job market. The Liberals, in particular, believe in the "Training Gospel." Frank MeKenna, the Liberal Premier of New Brunswick, was reported in the Globe and Mail as saying "If you have the training the jobs will take care of themselves."

One of the members of CANE went to a meeting at the University of Winnipeg during the Social Security Review. At that time Axworthy was the minister in charge. He turned up at the meeting. During the discussion he said to the assembled group "Do you remember that movie *Field of Dreams?* The line in the movie was 'Build it and they will come.' Well, if you have the training, the jobs will come." Regardless of the fact that thousands of well-trained and well-educated workers can no longer find work, the government's answer is to keep training people.

Not only do we have to endlessly be trained and re-trained for non-existent jobs, we have to be trained how to look for these jobs. Job finding clubs, whether run by the government or by private business, run on the same model. For the most part all job-finding clubs teach how to write a resume, network and find the hidden job market. But the most important thing they do is to "pump you up." You must be positive and have a good attitude. One of the stated goals of New Brunswick Works is to "change the attitude of the poor."

Jamie Swift says workers are treated like empty bottles that are constantly in need of refilling with skills, the hard skills for specific jobs and the soft skills for the right attitude.

The only exception I have discovered was the job-finding club run by the Grey Nuns. One of our members attended one of their sessions. It was the first time that we heard of someone having a good experience in a job-finding club. They apparently really cared about the people they were working with. People mattered.

In all the other job-finding clubs what mattered was getting a job, any job. The purpose of New Brunswick Works is to get people off social assistance and back to work. The training is the carrot. There is also the stick of punitive new social assistance regulations. The training, combined with hard work, has one goal, and that is to get people back into the market economy. There is one problem that is ignored. The jobs in the market economy are rapidly disappearing because of technological progress.

TECHNOLOGICAL PROGRESS

Some people worship technology. The new technology of the scientific age is everywhere. Everyday a new machine pops up. The other day for the first time I saw a machine selling stamps in one of the malls. The library is now full of machines. Not only are there machines to find books and magazines and magazine articles, there are now machines to check out books. There are also machines in the lobby that promise to find you jobs. The library has two new Employment Insurance machines to help us in our job search.

Every day a new machine does a job that a person used to do. I once asked one of the library clerks what he thought of the new check out machines. He thought they were a great idea! I was amazed at his reaction. I pointed out to him that the other day I had seen a line-up at the new machine while two human clerks stood waiting for someone to come and check out their books with them. How long before there are no longer any human check out clerks in the library?

Not only is the technological change escalating, this new technology is very different from the technology previous to the Industrial Revolution. The craftsman making a pot was using a holistic technology. Technology today is what Ursula Franklin calls "prescriptive technology." It is a technology linked to science. At the beginning of modern science was the idea that everything could be controlled. In order to have a scientific experiment you have to be able to control all the variables. It soon became clear that people were very difficult to control. There is only one way to control people. That is to make people into objects. We are now called human resources, and thus can be used like any other resource. Heather Menzies says that "Workers are 'post-it notes' that are stuck on where necessary and then discarded when no longer of any use."

In the Industrial Revolution all the objects, people included, were used to create a production line. On the production line everything is broken down into steps, and everything is controlled. Everyone used to be linked to production lines producing goods. I remember a summer job where I had to take unshelled peanuts off a conveyer belt. I had no control over how fast the belt was moving. I only lasted one day. The difference today in the Cybernetic Revolution is that production is less and less machine-based mass production. We now have computer based, information-intensive production. Now everyone is being linked up to computers. A 1995 Report of Statistics Canada tells us that 48% of workers are now working with or on computers.

George Grant talks about this new technology as being unique to our civilization. He links it to the religion of progress.

We now have " technological progress." This link of progress with a technology that focuses on planning and control has become so incredibly powerful that everyone seeks salvation through technological progress. Everyone from Marxist to liberal bows down to this god.

This is a god that we have all worshiped because we were promised liberation and prosperity. When sewing machines were invented, people thought that now everyone would have clothes. Just a few years ago everyone thought that new, improved technology would mean that everyone would work less and the problem would be what to do with our leisure time.

Instead we now are slaves to this new technology, to the new machines. In Manitoba these days we are told that we should be grateful that all these new telemarketing jobs are coming to our province. I was at a meeting the other day where people were planning a May Day March for Jobs. They were making a big telephone out of cardboard, and were going to chain people to it. Prescriptive technology leads to slavery of workers because it is based on control and planning.

As work is broken down into smaller and smaller tasks, more and more control is concentrated into fewer and fewer hands. People experience less and less decision making in their jobs. Jobs are deskilled and management takes more and more control. Someone who works for a large telecommunications company told me how frustrating his job is. He is always monitored and controlled and his performance is constantly judged. The control and deskilling can happen not only in one company, but it can happen in a whole community. Workers in Windsor, Ontario who once had skilled jobs are now semi-skilled and unskilled casino workers.[36]

It is not only concrete job decision-making that is lost. People also lose the ability to make judgments. Ursula Franklin believes that by its very nature prescriptive technology "eliminates decision making and judgment, especially for the making of principled decision." Gradually people become compliant in all aspects of their lives. We have developed a society of people who do not make decisions at work. Not only does the technology demand this, the bureaucratic institutions we have developed demand this. Then people come home from work and sit in front of the television where no decisions are required.

Finally, prescriptive technology not only leads to compliance and slavery, its underlying values combine with the god Growth. The underlying values are: whatever can be done should be done and everything that can be done should be done faster and faster. The cancer must be spread faster and faster. For George Grant the power of this god seems overwhelming. He saw a "tightening circle in which every hope betrays us and every attempt to wiggle free only tightens our bonds." But let us picture instead the big dumb giant running faster and faster. He is creating havoc everywhere. But David did defeat Goliath.

MAN ALONE

The final and most powerful god I have named Man Alone. *Man Alone* is the title of a collection of essays that was popular in the 1960s. At university we read this book and others that talked about the "alienation of man," not "persons" in those days. There was the awful vision of a person completely free and completely alone. It was considered a terrible tragedy to be alienated. It meant that one no longer belonged to society, that one no longer had a place. In a very short time there has been a complete change. Many people no longer seek a place in society. Rather they have accepted Margaret Thatcher's view that "there is no society." Now people seek to be totally alone and they call this freedom.

I use the word freedom in a very different way. The word freedom for me means the freedom that Martin Luther King sought. His vision of freedom was the same as the freedom sought by the slaves of Israel. The cry of Moses to the Pharaoh and the cry of King was "Let my people go!" Freedom movements have always been freedom for a group of people; freedom from an oppressive class, whether slave owners or the aristocracy of a country; or freedom from an oppressive political system, whether from the Right or the Left.

We now seek the god Man Alone, the freedom of the individual machine/object in the Monopoly game. We sometimes call this economic freedom because it reflects the goal of having a large amount of money. Money is sought partly to buy goods and services today, but more importantly to buy "economic freedom," which is to be able to buy goods and services today and forever. The money can come from anywhere. It is acceptable to obtain money by hard work, by birth or even by gambling. A lottery win is as acceptable as hard work. The people that run the lotteries know what people are really seeking when they buy the ticket. The advertising is quite clear. Lotto 6/49 says "Imagine the Freedom."

If we do not win a lottery, then we seek to enter the Monopoly game. We work hard to win this game. There are two strategies used to win. First we can compete with others . We are taught to compete by every institution in the society, including the school system. I remember when my son was in Grade Seven. He tried out for the basketball team. He went to every practice and worked really hard. He did not make the team. Another boy who seldom went to practice did. Because my son did not understand why this had happened, I went to the school. I asked the teacher why the decisions were made the way they were. She said that she was sorry, but the school personnel had discussed who would be on the team. They had decided that winning was more important than participation.

After school the competition gets even rougher. Thousands lose their businesses in the competitive market place. Thousands of people lose out in the job competition every day. Neither the winners, nor anyone else, has any responsibility for the losers. They are just winning what they deserve. The losers are just expected to try harder.

If the competition gets too fierce and it seems more prudent to make alliances, then we make contracts with each other. We have built a society based on contracts. Contracts assume free autonomous independent individuals making market decisions. If a society is only markets and economics, then running the society by contract makes sense. But it only makes sense as long as everyone is part of the market economy. Where does it leave all those outside? Non-employed people and children are outside the market economy. They have nothing to bargain with and no hope of signing a contract that will benefit them.

In a contract both sides have responsibilities. The belief of those committed to the market economy is that there are no responsibilities outside the contracts. Thus if I do not have a contract with you, then I am not responsible for you. It is obvious that many people have no contracts with anyone. Some have a marriage contract, but this contract is no longer a guarantee of some security, as it once was. So who is responsible for those without contracts? We used to believe in Canada that the government is responsible if no one else is willing to assume responsibility for an individual. This used to give Canadians some sense of security. We called it the Social Safety Net. We are told that we can no longer afford this. It is no wonder that people are afraid.

Only a few voices have been raised to challenge the idea that we no longer have any responsibility towards our neighbours. One of the few times there was a challenge to the lack of responsibility of government and of society was in response to the meeting of G7 countries in Halifax in 1996. The Canadian Council of Churches put out a document that stated we were leading our children to slavery, and that we now believed we were free from responsibility. I never saw any press coverage of this challenge.

The freedom of Man Alone is not only the freedom of no responsibility, it is the freedom of unlimited rights. Each person has the right to obtain what he or she wants, whenever he or she wants it. As Archbishop Camero states "if that means crushing a few, or many or numerous human beings, it is regrettable...but inevitable." Each person has the right to anything and everything: money; goods and services produced anywhere on the planet by any means; property, including intellectual property; natural resources, including patenting seeds and even DNA.

Everything is to be gained, but the question is never asked "At what price?"

MOLOCH

Any of the gods may be named Moloch. Moloch is a Hebrew name. It means "any influence which demands from us the sacrifice of what we hold most dear." At one time children were sacrificed on the flames of an alter. Now the sacrifice is not as dramatic. The sacrifice to the false gods is more quietly done behind closed doors. Often the people who demand the sacrifice have the best of intentions. "The road to hell is paved with good intentions."

Allen Ginsberg in *Howl* written in 1956 unmasked

Moloch for us.

Moloch, whose mind is pure machinery . . .
Moloch, whose blood is running money . . .
Moloch, whose love is endless oil and stone . . .
Moloch, whose soul is electricity and banks.

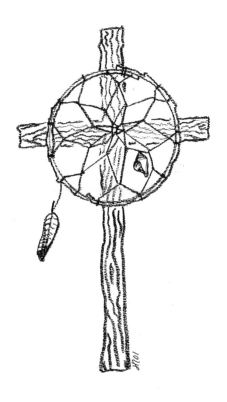

CHAPTER 7
I HAD NO CHOICE

*Ontario Finance Minister, Ernie Eves says he must slash
government programs in order to save them.*
GLOBE AND MAIL, JULY 21, 1995

*Industry Minister John Manley says, "the one weakness in the
Liberal election campaign was that they did not do a good
enough job explaining to Canadians that the Liberals had
cut the deficit to protect social programs."*
GLOBE AND MAIL, JUNE 6, 1997

D
URING THE 1984 FEDERAL ELECTION there was a televised debate between then Prime Minister John Turner and the Conservative Leader Brian Mulroney. For many people the election was decided after a riveting exchange between the two men over appointments that Turner had made. Mulroney pointed a finger at Turner accusing him of inappropriate political patronage. Turner responded by saying "I had no choice." He repeated it. "I had no choice." Could it be true that the most powerful person in Canada had no choice? Clearly at the time many Canadians did not believe this and chose to get rid of Turner.

Several elections have passed and now the feeling in the country is that no one has any choice about anything any more. Politicians and bureaucrats continue to tell us that there is no choice. When Winnipeg City Council was considering implementing user fees for the library I phoned my city councillor to voice my opposition. The answer his assistant gave me was "There is no choice." He asked if I would rather the library close. He was adamant that there was no choice. In other words there were only two choices, either the library closes or there are library fees. There must have been a third choice, because a year later neither had happened.

This continual bombardment from all levels of government that there is no choice is wearing us down. We are getting depressed. Depression comes when a person feels that they are in a box and that there is no way out. Depression comes when a person feels either that there are no alternatives to choose from, or that they have no power to implement the alternative they have chosen. In Canada today we now believe that there are no alternatives. We have accepted a number of myths, and the result is we are trapped in a box with no way out.

Boxes We Are In

I watched a program on cable television the other night. The topic was "How to get welfare people back to work." There was a panel of three people, all of whom were involved with Taking Charge. This is an excellent program for moms on welfare who want to upgrade their skills. The interviewer had a set notion in his head. People are on welfare because they do not have enough skills, either in order to do a job, or to find a job. When I phoned in to the show and said that half the people in CANE had university degrees and that the problem of people on welfare demands far more then skills upgrading, he dismissed my comments. He continued the pre-conceived theme of the show. I am sure this was not a stupid man. He was just ignorant of the real problems and resented the implication that he did not fully understand the situation.

The interviewer believed <u>Myth #1: There are jobs out there</u>. The longer version is: There is a job out there at a living wage for everyone, if they just try hard enough. This myth is repeated and reinforced over and over in and by the media. It is never questioned. Not only working people, but also the unemployed believe this myth. We are constantly told that new jobs are being created. This is true. But it is only half of the truth. Although jobs are continually being created, jobs are also continually being lost. Also the number of people in the labour force is continually increasing. Therefore the number of unemployed workers does not diminish. We still have one and a half million officially unemployed people. The society is not creating enough jobs for the work force. However, the myth that the society is creating enough jobs for everyone continues.

The result of this myth is that unemployment is considered to be the fault of the individual worker, not the society. This means that the solutions to unemployment usually focus on the individual worker and seldom on the society. If there really are enough jobs out there, then we can blame the ignorant and lazy worker on welfare, who really is not trying hard enough to get one of those jobs out there. This makes it acceptable to force people to work at below minimum wage at jobs for which they are unsuited. It is called Workfare. The result is pregnant women in New Brunswick clearing brush and unskilled workers in Alberta working at jobs that skilled, unionized health care workers once held.

Instead of Workfare, the government could establish job creation. This is seldom done by government because of <u>Myth #2: There is no money</u>. Occasionally, to my surprise, I read an article that shows this is a lie. A headline reads Average Canadian's Net Worth Higher by $1,900 Statistics Canada Shows.[37] The article is just talking about the increase for one year. The average net worth of Canadians went from $81,700 dollars in 1994 to $83,600 dollars in 1995. Not only that, the country's total wealth grew by 3.2% in 1995 to $2.8 trillion dollars. What this means in its simplest terms is that we are one of the richest countries in the world. And we are constantly told that there is no money.

Those who extol the virtues of trickle down economics continue to say that there is no money. We at the bottom are not getting any money trickling down because there is none available. We are told that this is not the fault of those at the top. They are working very hard to create a good economy for us, and one day we will all benefit. It is getting harder and harder to feed this line to the general public. We all read about bank profits and CEO salaries increasing and increasing. There does not seem to be an end to it. Maybe one day everyone will see that the wool was pulled over our eyes. Maybe one day we will all say it is not trickle down economics. It is vacuum cleaner economics, and the guys at the top are cleaning up.

Those who have all the money naturally want to keep it. Therefore, we have <u>Myth #3: We need less and less govern-ment interference in our lives.</u> Governments "interfere" in our lives in two ways. There are rules and regulations, and there is taxation. Over the years many rules and regulations have been brought into legislation dealing with all kinds of things such as the environment and workplace health and safety. These all have an impact on business. Those who extol the free enterprise system lobby government to get rid of all these rules that hinder their enterprises.

One of the most famous examples of free enterprise, that is, no government rules and regulations, happened in the United States. US President Ronald Reagan took off all the rules and regulations that governed the Savings and Loans (a form of small bank). They collapsed. Millions of people lost their savings. And the government was stuck with a bill in the billions of dollars to replace those savings.

Besides rules and regulations the government "interferes" in our lives through the tax system. The government takes some of the wealth of the country in order to do two things. First there is wealth re-distribution. We used to have a tax system that did a fairly good job in making sure that everyone had enough to live. The last twenty years has seen less and less re-distribution of income and wealth. It is well documented: the rich are getting richer and the poor are getting poorer.[38]

Second, taxes pay for services. I am happy to pay taxes in order to receive health, education and welfare services, also roads, sewers, libraries, etc. We not only get services, government services mean government jobs, usually well-paying, unionized government jobs. Now government services are declared inefficient and must be cut. The jobs, and consequently the services, are eliminated. Sometimes they are privatized. The media continues to reinforce the myth that government is inefficient and therefore privatization is a good thing.

Several years ago the Manitoba Conservative government was planning to privatize our parks. The CBC announced this. The commentary on this came from a person from the Chamber of Commerce, who extolled the virtues of business. It was said that business, of course, could do a much better job than government. Interestingly, government did a bad job because it was not interested in making a profit. I never really considered our parks as profit-making ventures before. I waited in vain for someone to comment from the opposite perspective. Someone could have spoken of parks as a resource for the community. No one did.

In order to redistribute wealth and to provide services

the government has to collect taxes. It does this in a variety of ways. We are all aware of the Goods and Services Tax (GST), a consumption tax that everyone pays. We are all aware of what we pay in income tax. What we are not aware of is what other people and corporations pay in income tax. Few people are aware of the massive changes that have occurred in Canadian taxation policy over the last twenty years. At one time corporations made up 50% of the tax base. Their share is now 6%. Individual tax changes, such as reducing the number of tax brackets to three, have reduced significantly the amount of taxes individuals at the top pay. These changes have meant less money collected and more money borrowed. Thus we have more government debt. Fifty percent of federal government debt was caused by taxation changes for upper income Canadians and for large corporations.[39]

The tax changes, plus high interest rates (44% of the federal government debt was caused by high interest rates) meant that the government amassed a huge debt. Now we have <u>Myth #4: The debt is the problem.</u> This myth was broadcast far and wide by every politician in the country. They failed to mention that debt is not a problem for the national government if the money is borrowed from the Bank of Canada. In that case we owe ourselves money. The most obvious example of a government incurring massive debt and then gradually paying it off with no adverse effects is the example of the debt incurred by WW II. It was far bigger then any debt any government now has. The debt has become a problem not because we borrowed money, but because the government has borrowed from the chartered banks and from outside the country. The true problem is that we borrowed money from the rich, instead of taxing the rich.

Finally, all the myths taken together combine to convince us of one thing. The biggest and most depressing myth of all is <u>Myth #5: The market economy has swallowed up the world, and there is nothing we can do about it.</u> No person or government can stop the inevitable tide of globalization and the free market economy. We are told that we have no choice. We are told that we just have to accept this incredibly depressing state of affairs. It is no wonder that people give up, keep their head down, and hope they can survive for another day.

The truth is that we have the power to open the boxes. We can unmask the lies that have made us believe that there are no choices. Once we know that there are choices, we need to know where the power in the society really lies, so that we can implement the choices that we want.

Knowledge is Power

When we have discussions at CANE about how the society works most people have a very fuzzy idea of where the power lies. When explaining our democratic system I usually start with the preceding diagram:

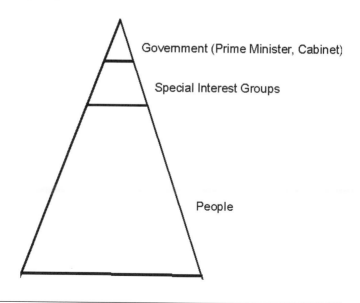

Government (Prime Minister, Cabinet)

Special Interest Groups

People

The government makes the rules that the rest of us have to live by. [*see* pyramid chart *on page 121*]

At the top we have the Prime Minister who, it has been said, is "elected as dictator every four years." Prime Minister Chretien certainly sees himself as the decision-maker for the country. In his entertaining off the cuff remarks to the Belgian Prime Minister at the NATO Conference in July 1997 he compared our system to the US system. He can decide to make a deal, but US President Clinton has to appease 53 groups and committees. In Canada, a Prime Minister with a majority government need not consult with anyone. In a letter to the Globe and Mail, July 16, 1997, the writer commenting on Chretien's remarks calls this "democratic dictatorship."

However, the Prime Minister does not make decisions in a vacuum. He or she names a cabinet. Russ Doern, in his book *Wednesdays are Cabinet Days*, says there is nothing democratic about the cabinet form of government. He was an NDP MLA for fifteen years, and a Minister for seven. Doern served in a provincial cabinet, but both federally and provincially the process is the same. The Leader selects the Cabinet. One can debate whether this is the best form of democratic government or not. Nevertheless, it is what we have at the moment.

Within any cabinet there is, of course, a variety of opinion and emphasise. However, all cabinet members are members of the same political party. All share that party's interpretation of reality, its goals, and its overall strategy to reach its goals. As in any group, the group members influence decisions, and the leader both reflects and influences the decisions made by the group. Together, the Leader and the other members of the Cabinet decide what kind of society we will all live in.

The media identifies differences within any Cabinet. The perception of the Liberal federal Cabinet is that there are both left-leaning and right-leaning members. Lloyd Axworthy, who was the MP for Winnipeg South Centre, has always been depicted as a left-leaning Liberal who cared about social programs. When he was the Minister for the Department of Human Resources the massive cuts to social programs intensified. Because of our perception of Axworthy this was hard for us in Winnipeg, indeed in the rest of the country, to understand. I remember Mary Walsh as Marg Delahunty, from the television show *This Hour has 22 Minutes*, interviewing Axworthy. She obviously thought that he was not the instigator of the cuts, but rather that he had lost the battle in Cabinet over the cuts. She pleaded with him not to give in to the right wing agenda. "My darling, don't let them do this to you." We do not know who said what in Cabinet when these decisions were made. However, every member of Cabinet had a choice. Axworthy could support the measures or resign.

The choice was made by all members of Cabinet and then sold to the Canadian people by saying they had no choice. This strategy is carried out by governments at both the federal and provincial levels. Both governments continually say, with a straight face, that the destruction of Canada's social safety net is the inevitable result of deficit cutting. It is really too bad, but there is no alternative. On the other hand, they know that we do not like to have all the programs that have taken seventy years to build be destroyed. So they say that they are doing this in order to save the social programs. Ed Finn, on reflecting on this "double-speak," says that Canadians now believe that the Liberals don't want to pick on the poor and helpless, but there is no alternative.[40]

Although the Prime Minister and the Cabinet make the decisions and have the final authority, there are others who influence the decisions that are made. Their political party influences in many ways. There are the party's back benchers, those in the party's hierarchy who have access and influence, and political staff. Each member of parliament has staff. The Prime Minister's staff has always had incredible power. One does not hear much about the Prime Minister's Office (the PMO) these days. I remember in Trudeau's days as Prime Minister that the power this group had was bitterly resented by ordinary Liberal back benchers.

Finally, all governments are influenced, to a greater or less extent, by the bureaucracy of government, the civil service. These people remain in place making sure everything carries on regardless of which political party is in power. As in every bureaucracy, there is the inevitable resistance to change. Any minister who wants to bring about change in his or her department has to be firmly in control. I remember having lunch one day with Al Mackling, who had been a Provincial NDP Cabinet Minister for many years. He was talking about how hard it was to change things. If he wanted to do things differently his staff would show him why this could not be done. One day he was fed up. He called them in, banged on his desk and said that he wanted an outline by the next week of how the changes could be implemented. The next week the proposed changes were on his desk. Sometimes the role has power only if the person is willing to exercise it.

Special Interest Groups

It is important and necessary to consult any group who will be affected by government policy. It is ruinous to let any group dictate government policy.

The most effective special interest group in Canada today is a group that came together nearly twenty-five years ago, and that has, since that time, worked quietly and effectively to lobby government. This group has had remarkable, indeed spectacular success. It is the corporate business group. Not only in Canada, but all over the world, the heads of multi-national corporations got together and formed their special interest groups. First there was the Business Round Table in the United States. The heads of forty-two out of fifty of the top "Fortune 500" companies came together.

In 1976 the Canadian version was born. It is called the Business Council on National Issues (BCNI). The BCNI is made up of the 160 largest corporations in Canada, controlling over one trillion dollars in assets. Membership is by invitation only. The focus of the group is on federal policy. Its high profile members have access to the most powerful politicians and civil servants in the country. Its goal is to directly influence economic, fiscal and social policy. Its success has been staggering. The Mulroney government position on trade, taxation, defence and monetary policy was virtually identical to the position papers produced by the BCNI.[41] The group continues to influence government policy. At the August, 1997 Premiers' Conference a position paper on national unity was presented to the Premiers. The principles were similar to those of the Reform Party. Spokesmen for Reform Party Leader Preston Manning and Intergovernmental Affairs Minister Stephane Dion welcomed the BCNI approach. What other group has such access to government?

The BCNI is not alone in its lobbying efforts. There are other business groups. One is the Alliance of Manufacturers and Exporters of Canada (AMEC). With a $6.5 million dollar operating budget, the organization promotes free trade, lower wages and reduced social benefits for workers. There is also the Canadian Bankers' Association (CBA) which justifies bank profits. As well as these organizations there are also other so-called "grass roots" organizations. Each group has a slightly different focus, but all have the same free enterprise agenda. There is the National Citizens' Coalition, which campaigned vigorously against the introduction of Medicare and the Canada Health Act. There is also the Canadian Taxpayers Federation, which runs anti-tax campaigns, and the National Firearms Association.

Business special interest groups lobby government, but they also work to change public opinion. When legislation is put forward by the federal government, these groups begin their lobbying of government and their media campaigns to influence the general public. The year before the business community set up the BCNI, a small group of powerful BC executives got together to create a think-tank in order to counter-act the threat of the "socialist," that is NDP, government in BC. They brought in Michael Walker as Executive Director. He told his backers "If you really want to change the world you have to change the ideological fabric of the world." And he set up the Fraser Institute.[42]

The Fraser Institute, together with the Public Policy Forum and the C.D. Howe Institute, has made major advances towards the goal of changing a people's ideology or conventional wisdom. These groups are not called special interest groups. They are called "independent think tanks." They all have a similar agenda, or strategy, but they have different tactics. For example, the C.D. Howe Institute has led the attack on Canada's social programs and the hysteria over the deficit.[43]

One of the main funders of all these organizations is the Donner Canadian Foundation. It began in 1953 funding a variety of charitable organizations. Although the focus was always right wing, a major change happened in 1993 when Devon Cross became the President. She said that she intended to create a national network of new conservatives, and she has done so.

Under Cross the Donner Canadian Foundation dispersed $2 million dollars annually.[44]

The Fraser Institute reaches out to the general public in a number of ways. There are books and conferences and contests. For example, there are contests on how to re-structure government. In 1992 the Federal Minister of State for Finance awarded the prizes. The Finance Minister, Paul Martin, has also presented the awards to the winners. There is also a systematic focus on young people. There are Fraser Institute Student Seminars on Policy Issues held across the country. The most promising students are chosen to participate in Fraser Institute Student Leader's Colloquium where they learn the free market ideology.

There has been only one noticeable exception to the success of these groups. The National Firearms Association, with help from the United States National Rifle Association, was not able to prevent the Liberal government from bringing in gun registration. In this case there were enough other groups, such as women's groups, to pressure the government to bring in gun control.

We all recognise that competing special interest groups influence government policy. If all these groups had equal access to government and there was informed debate on the issues this would be a good thing. However the perception of the public seems to be that special interest groups are a bad thing. I puzzled over this, because it seems like such a good thing to join together with others for a common cause.

People have power when they join together with others of like mind. This is a perfectly logical and legitimate thing to do. Workers join together in unions of all kinds, and the unions join together to create the Canadian Labour Congress. Women join together in a variety of groups from REAL Women to the

National Action Committee on the Status of Women. People with disabilities, mental or physical, join together with others of similar disabilities and with family, friends and caregivers. There are groups of people who share an ethnic or cultural background. There are groups who struggle to become a nation within a nation; Aboriginal and Quebecois. Each group lobbies government to make the rules that will help them reach their objectives. This is how our democracy works.

So how is it that special interest groups are considered a bad thing? The reason they are perceived as a bad thing, is because special interest groups are considered "self-interest groups." Any government that does not want to listen to the demands of a group of people immediately labels them a special interest group (read self-interest group). The general public then perceives the group as only caring about their own members. Ralph Klein did this very effectively in Alberta in his fight against public sector unions.

Any group that seeks to influence government policy has its own special interests. The question that has to be asked is who defines the public interest? What do the people want? Who are the people?

The People
In a democracy, the power lies with the people.

When I think of "the people" I remember the people fighting for and winning the battle to bring Medicare to Manitoba. Tommy Douglas and the CCF had initiated first Hospitalization, and then Medicare in Saskatchewan. The Liberals under Lester Pearson then decided to legislate the National Health Act which brought in Medicare as a joint program with the provinces. Each province then had to decide whether they would join. The funding would be 50/50. At the time we had a Conservative government in Manitoba. They steadfastly refused to implement Medicare. A Citizen's Group to Bring Medicare to Manitoba was formed. I was a young social work student and found myself on the Executive of the group. I clearly remember first the marches, and then going to legislative hearings. The Minister of Health was George Johnson. The speakers, one after another, from all walks of life and from a multitude of groups, demanded that the provincial government join with the federal government in implementing Medicare. The Conservatives finally accepted the wishes of the people, and implemented the legislation.

When my daughter Catharine thinks of "the people" she thinks of the national referendum on the Charlottetown Accord. All the elites of the country, all the political parties, all the authorities said to vote one way and the people chose another way. Our family watched as the results came in and cheered. After it was over Catharine said she now had renewed faith in the people.

In the case of the Charlottetown Accord, the people dug in their heels and said "no" to the authorities. In the case of the battle for Medicare, the people demanded those in authority give them what they wanted. There was a positive force of thousands of individuals united in a common cause. The cause was one that benefited the whole community. There has not been such a coming together of the people in common cause for a clear objective since those battles of the 1960s. There have been demonstrations against all the terrible devastation, primarily caused by the federal government, in the last ten years, but the government carries on with its plans. For the most part the public protests have not worked. The majority of the people have been convinced that there is no alternative.

However, no matter how much propaganda is fed to

people in order to convince them that it is all for their own good, you still cannot fool all the people all the time. There was a women's march in Quebec which had clear objectives that were obtained. If people are truly hurting from government policy, and it is clear that it is government policy, they will vote against the government. In Atlantic Canada the cuts to Employment Insurance were so horrendous that the people decided to "throw the rascals out" and to elected Conservatives and New Democrats in 1997. It is interesting that although people are still seeking alternatives, there is no consensus on what the alternative should be. During the 1990s Canadians were as likely to vote for the Reform Party as to vote for the NDP in order to change things.

There is a lack of understanding of how the world works, of what kind of society we want and how to achieve it. This means that the people are losing the power to fight for a common cause. Murray Dobbin has given a clear concise analysis of how the people have lost their power. He describes how the Left accepted a linear view of society that assumed progress would continue. The focus was more and more on rights, and less and less on "economic and social democracy issues." The status quo, including a demeaning and destructive welfare system, was accepted, and there was no push for tax reform. The popular movements became bureaucratized and dependent on government money. Howard Adams shows how this was done with the Native Movements.[45]

The people became less and less literate in the area of social and economic development and policy. People assumed our social programs had always been there, and forgot the battles to win them. Dobbin calls this "historical amnesia." We know less and less of our history. Canadian history is no longer compulsory in most provincial high schools. It is not only that people lack knowledge of their history. The conventional wisdom of the society has changed. What was once a lunatic fringe idea now is considered common sense. There is another term we sometimes use instead of conventional wisdom or common sense. When conventional wisdom becomes a faith statement it becomes an ideology. Then no amount of logical evidence can contradict an ideology. The ideology we hold justifies what we do. There is nothing more powerful. For an ideology is held implicitly and it is "adopted as a whole regardless of the course of events." People seldom use the term ideology these days. We are more likely to talk about a world view.

Who Puts Us to Sleep?

What we read in our newspapers and magazines, what we hear on the radio and see on television, all combine to present a world view. The media both present and influence our view of the world. Someone has decided what that should be. We usually are aware of the reporters, and only vaguely aware of the editors. But behind both are the owners of the media. The issue of ownership of the media became prominent when Conrad Black began buying up newspapers in Canada. There was a loud outcry from many people and organizations who recognized that this is a bad thing. It is a bad thing in general for one person to have such control over what people think. It is a particularly bad thing when that person is Conrad Black. We have seen what Black has done in other countries. In Israel he bought the *Jerusalem Post* shifting its editorial policy dramatically to the right.[46] political climate was shifted to the right. In Canada we now have the *National Post*.

The issue is not only ownership of the media. There is a constant flow of information that is sent to and used by the media. For example, there are thousands of column inches in newspapers, and constant editorials using Fraser Institute material as a resource. In addition to the articles criticising government policy, the Fraser Institute puts out a government report card which is featured in many daily newspapers. At the same time that the Fraser Institute is inundating the media with its own information, it is putting out studies that show the media is hostile to big business. Its National Media Archive publishes its findings in *On Balance: Media Treatment of Public Policy Issues*. These studies attempt to prove that big business is unfairly treated.

My closing thought on the Fraser Institute is one that Michael Valpy expressed He said "those people will leave no stone unturned in their determination to recreate a feudal peasant class feeding on roots."[47]

How We Are Put To Sleep

As Ed Finn said in the June 1997 edition of *Canadian Forum* "Our corporate rulers don't need concentration camps to imprison our bodies, so long as they have the media apparatus to imprison our minds."

We live in the Information Age. What this means is that we have so much information that we do not know what to do with it all. We are constantly bombarded by an overwhelming amount of stimuli. The news of the day never stops. All this information has to be reduced to a manageable level, or we would go crazy. We know how this happens through the writings of Noam Chomsky, who writes about transformational grammar. It is a vast subject, but some of his key ideas help us understand how we deal with all this information. He explains that we take information in, and then generalize, delete and distort it in order to make sense of things. However, even before we get the information the media have already engaged in this process. We tend to accept the generalizations, deletions and distortions that the media feed us, because we just do not have the time to sift through everything and to come to our own understanding.

The generalizations that the media feed to us are the myths. The 30 second sound bite is the perfect vehicle for constant repetition of the myths. They are repeated over and over again until they are accepted without question. As we have come to accept the myths, we are now trapped in the boxes that they create.

Deletions and distortions are most evident when we are dealing with numbers. What is counted and how we count is crucial. People have always understood that statistics, by themselves, out of context, can prove anything. Mark Twain spoke of "lies, damn lies, and statistics."

One of the most obvious examples of a number giving a half truth is the Statistics Canada unemployment figures. According to Statistics Canada, there are one and a half million Canadians officially unemployed. However, large groups of people are not counted and are not considered unemployed. Discouraged workers who have given up looking are not counted. Part-time workers who want full-time work are not counted. Treaty Indians are not counted. The under-employed, those with a university degree working at a McJob are not counted. Contract workers, those who have a job for two or three months are not counted. The Canadian Centre for Policy Alternatives estimated Canada's real jobless rate at 20%.

It is not only numbers, but the meaning of words that are distorted. Reform once meant making things better. Words are distorted by adding descriptive adjectives that change their meaning. We now have phrases such as: bloated work force, whining special interest groups, tax burden, debt crisis, etc.

Finally, by substituting new words for previous words,

new realities are created. The people are turned into "taxpayers" and "consumers" instead of citizens. On one episode of *Face Off* on CBC Newsworld, Rick Salutin and John Crispo were debating what to call people. Salutin maintained that if you call people taxpayers this impoverishes their identity and strips their citizenship. If you call people consumers this means that the business model has triumphed. Crispo responded by saying "but everything I do is consuming goods and services."

Here, in Winnipeg, our former mayor Susan Thompson considered the people "customers." Thus, everything is a market transaction. People who go to the library are "library customers." The sign at the Tax Branch at City Hall now reads Customer Service. We are now customers of municipal services, not citizens interacting with our government.

It is not only numbers and words, but whole articles that are distorted. Relevant facts are deleted. Robert and I were talking about this process over coffee at the Salisbury House coffee shop one Saturday morning. I said that I needed an example, so we decided to look at that morning's Saturday paper. We opened up the August 16, 1997 Winnipeg Free Press and read the editorial. There was a discussion on privatizing Winnipeg Hydro. At first glance the editorial gave the impression of being fair, and of looking at both sides. We are told that Winnipeg Hydro makes $15 million dollars each year. Then the other side is presented. We are told that Winnipeg Hydro probably needs $300 million dollars to fix and upgrade its plants. This means money has to be borrowed and, according to the Free Press, this could effect Hydro's credit rating and profitability. However, they fail to say that upgrading facilities is part of normal business practice. Any business takes ongoing depreciation into account. By deleting such significant facts the reader is led to believe that it would be a good thing to sell off a utility that earns the City of Winnipeg $15 million dollars a year.

After the media have finished putting together the "facts" for us, the final step is to communicate the information to us. Chomsky explains how we are put into a trance state by the use of presuppositions. The presuppositions define the discussion. They define what we can talk about. The most famous example is "Have you stopped beating your wife yet?"

Initially the presuppositions are invisible. Media, politicians, bureaucrats use them continually, but we are not aware of them. However, once you get sensitized to this technique, the examples leap out at you. A reporter will ask someone "What is the most effective way to get tough on crime?" This pre-supposes that the solution is to "get tough" on crime, rather than focussing on the causes of crime. We are effectively locked into a discussion on crime that focuses on "getting tough." Fortunately, once we do realize what is happening we can break out of those boxes.

I was at a conference put on by a group of Aboriginal women. It was held at the Indian and Metis Friendship Centre. Some government politicians and bureaucrats were invited to speak. One senior provincial government bureaucrat began to tell us about the exciting research that her department was engaged in. They had decided that teen pregnancy was a problem. For the last two years they had been trying to determine why teens were getting pregnant, and how they could stop this from happening. This state of affairs had to stop because it was so unhealthy for the young women and their children. She, unfortunately, had to report to us that after two years they still did not have the answers. When questions were invited from the floor, I got up. I said "The reason why you have not found the answer is because you are asking the wrong question. The right question is: How do you create healthy families?" There was a great round of applause. I had broken the presupposition. The box was opened.

It is not only the presuppositions that put us into a trance state. There is another technique that is detailed for us by Richard Bandler and John Grinder in their writings on Neuro-Linguistic Programming (NLP). They begin with the assumption that our ideologies are pretty chaotically organized. From countless discussions on social issues with a wide range of people, I would agree with this assumption. Precisely because people do not think through their ideology, and it is more chaotic than logical, ideology can be changed. One way it can be changed is by the technique of "pace, pace, lead." You pace the person you are giving information to, that is, you give a fact or idea that he or she agrees with. Next you pace again and give another fact that he or she agrees with. Then you lead. You give a third fact. There may be no logical connection, however, chances are the person will accept the third statement.

Let me give an example of how this is done. I came across a story concerning France's unemployment situation.[48] They have an official unemployment rate of 12.6%. The article begins by stating that France is in a dire need of more jobs. Everyone agrees. (pace) The article continues and we read that most French executives say radical labour market changes are needed. We agree. (pace) The executives then say that the solution is more cuts to welfare payments and more freedom to fire employees. (lead) There is no logical connection between the second statement and the third. But the reader has been gently led. The last statement will be considered, and if repeated enough times will be accepted by many.

To go back to our example of the privatization of our parks. We are told that parks need more money. (pace) We are told that everyone wants the parks to stay open. (pace) Then we are told that the answer is privatization. (lead) The answer has no logical connection to the initial statements. Not only that, there is only one answer given to the problem. In the story there is no alternative to the third statement. The answer given to the public will be considered, and if repeated enough times, will be accepted by enough people so that the government will say they are only doing what the people want. And they will end by saying they had no choice.

Choices We Make

Choices are made by politicians every day. Usually we, the people, have no idea how those choices are made. However, occasionally the process is documented, and we have the opportunity to see how the choices were made, by who, and why. Thanks to Jim Silver, who wrote *Thin Ice: Money, Politics, and the Demise of an N.H.L. Franchise* we have such an opportunity. The book outlines the massive free-for-all battle to "Save the Jets."

In the concluding chapter Silver first asks the question, "How are choices made, and who makes them?" He then gives us the answers. He concludes that two special interest groups put intense pressure on the politicians to "save" the Winnipeg Jets. The first and most significant was the corporate business sector. Both local corporate leaders, plus broader corporate forces, put incredible effort into forcing all levels of government to put money into the coffers of the Jets owners. Not only government but ordinary citizens were asked to contribute money. The other group supporting the Jets was a small, but vocal portion of the public. These people were, as Silver says, "almost rabid" in their determination. The two groups were buoyed by the media. The media was happy to showcase the Save the Jets rallies. The quick visuals and the thirty second sound bites filled our minds. There was no evaluation of the complex economic ramifications.

According to polls, the majority of the public did not favour spending millions of dollars to Save the Jets, but their opposition was passive and not focussed. Even organized labour was split on the issue. Some feared loss of money in the public sector and thus loss of jobs. Others wanted the jobs that would come from building a new arena. If it were not for the small group called Thin Ice there would not have been any focussed opposition. The politicians continued to listen to the two special interest groups, and continued to vote to give the Jets millions of dollars. They did this even though they had reports that showed that the Jets were not financially viable. Finally the project collapsed. The corporate sector was not willing to put sufficient money into the project.

My most memorable discussion concerning the Jets was with my friend Peter Williams, who was the minister at Young United Church. Young shared space at Crossways with CANE and other community groups. One day I listened to Peter explain how the City of Winnipeg refused to help the Youth Outreach program at Crossways. One hundred kids came there every day. There is no money for the children, but there is money for the Jets. Peter asked, "Where are our priorities?"

The politicians continue to make the choices. We, the people, have the power to make sure they make the choices that reflect our priorities.

CHAPTER 8

GRUBBING FOR GARBAGE

Charity today means condescending, heartless giving in order to be free of the sight of misery. Aid so given produces hatred and the recipient is not so much helped, as humiliated.
GUSTAVE WEIGEL, S.J., *The Dorothy Day Book*

We entrust charities with money to feed the poor, but we do not put money into the hands of the poor so they can feed themselves.
MARLENE WEBBER, *Food for Thought*

I WAS ONCE WITNESS to an interesting exchange between some Aboriginal women and a Minister of Native and Northern Affairs in the Manitoba Provincial Government. The Minister, David Newman, had come to speak and to bring greetings from the Province to this group of women. They had gathered at the Indian and Metis Friendship Centre in order to talk about their lives of grinding poverty, and what they could do to bring about change. After the minister spoke there was time for questions. The director of the Women's Transition Centre, an agency that provided a temporary home for abused women, got up to ask a question. She spoke about changes in government policy on social assistance. She pointed out that there was no longer special needs money available. The result was that when women left an abusive relationship they had no money to start up a new household. They used to be able to receive money from the

Province to buy basic necessities like a bed. Now this money was no longer there. The result was women and children sleeping on the floor. What did the Minister propose to solve this problem?

The Minister was stumped for a minute, but he quickly recovered. He said he had a good idea. Many people in the suburbs had mattresses and other things that could be used. Therefore we could have a giant garage sale with these items in order to help these women. A young native woman stood up and said "We don't want your garbage." The Minister, never at a loss for words, quickly replied "Yes, you are right. We need quality control."

The coordinator of the event, Suzanne, then spoke in words of eloquence and with great passion. She spoke of the need for justice for her people. She said, "We tell you of our untold suffering, despair and destitution, and your answer is a garage sale." Such answers are not good enough, and never will be.

And yet, Newman was well-meaning and wishing to help. There are many people in out communities who sincerely wish to help the less fortunate. For example, I know a United Church located in Winnipeg's inner city. They considered their outreach to the community to be their yearly garage sale. The garage sale has many positive sides to it. They are raising money for their church. In fact, it is one of the biggest money makers of the year. Raising money for the church is a good thing. They are also recycling things that they no longer have a use for. Recycling is a good thing.

Recycling clothes, furniture and household goods, even recycling computers, is a good thing. Our society is far too wasteful! The people and organizations who do this are usually private charities like churches, or the Goodwill or the Diabetes

Society. It is a win-win situation. Money is raised for charity, and goods are recycled. In fact, it is such a good money maker that the business is booming. More and more, and bigger and bigger is the used goods business.

The people on a limited income benefit. So why were the people at the Friendship Centre so enraged? Money and goods have always been given by the rich to the poor. In this transaction the poor are sometimes grateful, and are expected to be grateful. More and more this expected gratitude is transformed into rage or sullen depression. There are two reasons why this is so. The first is that today in Canada the goods and money received from all sources, either private charity or public funding, is woefully inadequate. When we started CANE in 1993 this was not the case. Most people were managing at a destitution level. Their position was that they would rather starve than go to a food bank. However, in 1996 the Conservative government in Manitoba made another cut in welfare payments. They said it was a 10% cut, but there was no cut to the rent paid to landlords. Since rent is about half of what the monthly payment is, the outcome was a 20% cut in food and personal needs. Single people now get a total monthly payment of $411 dollars to cover food, rent, personal needs and whatever else is necessary to live. After the cut I saw people struggling to manage, and then losing the struggle. The choice now is literally go to the food bank or starve.

There is another issue just as important as the amount of money. The relationship between the givers and the receivers, the haves and the have-nots depends on how the money and resources are given

There are three different kinds of relationships between givers and receivers. There are three different kinds of bonds between the people of Canada.[49]

---

1) BOND: COVENANT

The covenant, or contract between the Canadian people has been based on the idea that all citizens in this country have rights. The rights apply equally to all citizens. No one has the power to judge another, or to take away the rights of another. These rights are the rights of the Canadian welfare state. The word "welfare" has now become a dirty word, so rather than use the word welfare, we can talk about justice, and the rights of the Canadian citizen.

At the turn of the century laissez-faire capitalism, or the monopoly game became the dominant economic system. At the same time there were counter-forces calling for justice for those left out of the game. Gradually a movement arose in Canada which was led by people who had a particular understanding of the Christian gospel. The Social Gospel Movement was led by people such as J.S. Woodsworth, Tommy Douglas, and Stanley Knowles. They joined forces with farmers, intellectuals and labour to form the CCF and later the NDP. They believed that society had to identify and put into law people's rights. There was no judgment of the individual. Rather every person's basic needs had to be met.

The first modern social program was implemented in 1926 after a deal was struck between Liberal Prime Minister McKenzie King and J.S.Woodsworth. King invited Woodsworth over for supper and offered him the post of Minister of Labour. Woodsworth refused, but agreed to support King's minority government if King would implement Old Age Pensions and relief for the unemployed.

Gradually more and more universal programs were enacted. Tommy Douglas implemented Hospitalization and Medicare in Saskatchewan. Finally, in the 1960s the federal Liberals, in conjunction with the provinces brought in universal health care. In Manitoba the Conservative government agreed to bring in Medicare after a huge protest by ordinary Manitobans. We demanded universal health care as a right for all citizens, and we succeeded in pressuring the government to enact the necessary legislation. I remember being at the legislative committee meetings. We were determined to win.

In the 1960s there was another major contract legislated by government for all citizens. This was the Canada Assistance Plan or CAP. It also was a federal/provincial agreement. Two important components were the 50/50 cost sharing agreement and the five rights that were spelled out in the act. Our governments stated in law that we had the right to 1) an income 2) an adequate income 3) the right to appeal decisions made about our income 4) the right not to have to work or train for that income 5) there be no residency requirements to obtain income.

Most people think that our rights were enshrined in the Canadian Charter of Rights and Freedoms. Unfortunately, the charter only says that we have a right to food and shelter. In practice this only means that we have a right to food banks and hostels. Although there has been some attempt to interpret the charter to mean a right to an adequate standard of living, the courts so far have not interpreted the charter in this way.

In the 1980s another covenant was signed by the Canadian government. This covenant was signed by Brian Mulroney. Although the Conservative government signed the UN Covenant on Economic, Social, and Cultural Rights, the covenant was not enacted in legislation. Therefore, the Canadian government does not legally have to honour it. However, the Canadian government has to report to the UN every five years, and we have to show how we are doing. Up until the CAP Agreement was unilaterally terminated by the federal government in the February 1996 budget, the Canadian government always pointed to CAP to show how well we were looking after our people.

At the same time that Canadian governments were enacting rights for Canadians, they were putting programs into place that meant the rights were implemented. What is interesting is that only some Canadians had their right to an adequate income actually implemented. Those who could not reasonably take part in the labour market, most notably our senior citizens, were given enough money to live on. The people, and thus the politicians, decided that our senior citizens had worked hard all of their lives. They deserved to retire in dignity. First there was the Old Age Pension and then the Guaranteed Income Supplement. The supplement is needs tested through the income tax system. Any bureaucratic assessment is strictly related to one's income, not to one's moral character. The elderly are not expected to work to receive their money. They receive their money because they are Canadian citizens.

Children also are not considered part of the labour force. The society decided that they had a right to money, so that they could grow up as healthy productive citizens. We enacted the Family Allowance, another universal program. When the amount was deemed not adequate, there was a major increase under the Trudeau Liberals. The money I received for my three children when they were small made a big difference to our family. I remember our US relatives being utterly amazed that the government sent every family in the country $24 dollars per child.

There was also a universal program for those in the work force. It was called Unemployment Insurance and it covered most working Canadians. Up until the 1980s, UI was there for workers who lost their jobs, and for seasonal workers.

Other programs were put into place for those of working age who could not participate in the work force. Programs were implemented by provinces for people considered disabled, and thus "unemployable." However, the biggest group on provincial welfare was mothers with children under 18 years of age. These mothers and children had to be provided for, but it was done grudgingly, and at a minimum level of assistance. The children of these parents grew up in poverty.

Finally, there is the category of "employable" workers. These people are considered capable of working and are expected to find work. Municipal governments usually have been responsible for this group of citizens. There have been social workers and job-finding clubs available to help re-integrate these workers into the labour force. It was assumed they were responsible adults who required extra assistance as well as money to live on. It was up to the individual whether they availed themselves of the help offered.

All these programs were put into place by the three levels of Canadian government, and paid for by the taxes collected by the government. Everyone was entitled to the programs. Everyone paid for the programs. It was understood that the taxes we paid went to pay for the social programs we expected to have available for all. The governments were responsible for this covenant between the Canadian people because only the state can guarantee rights. The citizens of Canada used to take all our social programs as a given, our right as Canadians. Politicians used to call them "a sacred trust." We have forfeited our right with scarcely a whimper. We have sold our birthright, not for a bowl of porridge, but for an empty bowl. We have gained nothing.

2) BOND: CONSTRAINT
In archaic usage the word bond was a noun for slavery. The

meaning was expanded to mean anything that took away one's liberty, anything that made one feel trapped and powerless. This bond is the bond of the charitable institution. The most obvious example is the food bank. A few years ago things were so bad that I decided that the time had come to go to a food bank. First I had to phone them to find out where and when I could go. I discovered that I could go to the Unitarian church not far from our house. I steeled myself for the ordeal. I set off walking to the church and when I arrived I saw an old friend giving out the food. We were both social workers by profession. We had worked together on many committees, marched together in the 1960s and still met whenever there was an event where concerned people gathered. This made it worse. If the "helper" who gave out the food had been a stranger I would not have felt so bad. But he was now the "helper" and I was the "helped." I was now a "charity case." And as Marlene Webber says "Subtle shaming is endemic to charity." I never went back.

There is one other alternative. It is begging. Who would ever have thought that here in Canada, one of the richest countries in the world, there would be beggars. A friend of ours was talking to Robert about beggars. She said that she never wanted to go to India, because she would not be able to stand seeing all the people begging for money. But now that is the norm in Canada. People respond to the beggars in various ways. Some people will stop and give change to the beggars. Some people give money if the beggars are "working" at something such as playing an instrument. Some people are frightened and hurry on by.

I sometimes stop and talk to people who are begging on the street. My experience has been that they are determined to keep their self-respect. That may seem like a funny thing to say, but begging is better than going to a food bank or to welfare. They prefer to have some freedom in their lives. I talked to a woman outside Harry's Foods where I shop. She was asking for money. I thought I would try to be helpful so I told her about how she could get food from the food bank. She thanked me, and said that she preferred to ask people for money. At the food bank there is no choice in what you get. She would rather beg for money, and then go into Harry's and buy what food she wanted. She was fighting to retain that little bit of choice that was still open to her. I guess she had not heard or accepted the phrase "beggars can't be choosers."

There never is a choice when one depends on food banks or on Christmas hampers. The basic assumption is that other people choose your food for you. The same things go into every Christmas hamper. We had a lot of sugar for our coffee at CANE after Christmas. Everyone got sugar in their hampers. But a number of people do not use white sugar in coffee, or anything else. So they brought it in to share with those of us who do use sugar. It would have been nice if they could have had a choice in what they received. They could have received something that they could use.

What do people usually get from food banks? It is totally arbitrary. It depends on what the food industry is overloaded with on any particular day. "Wholesalers and retailers lay out hard cash for trucking and dumping edible food they don't sell. By contrast, it costs them next to nothing when food bank volunteers load and cart away garbage. That garbage consists mostly of stale dated, mislabeled or cosmetically imperfect nonperishables, as well as production overruns."[50] At CANE we often throw out fruits and vegetables that are no longer usable. I was talking to one of the volunteers at the food bank down the road. I asked him what he thought of the food. He said they had to throw out half the potatoes they received this week, because they were so rotten the bags were full of liquid running off the rotten potatoes.

Not all the food is coming from the business community. Some of the food is coming from generous people who want to help. They put tins into containers at stores. They take food to events such as hockey games. This type of giving depends on the individual's inclination, spare time and money this week. However, as Michael Volpey says in one of his columns "sharing should not depend on who feels like sharing."

Do the helpers always feel like sharing? Unfortunately, there is a syndrome called "donor burnout." Although Canadians can be very generous, as the problem goes on and on with no end in sight, the donations get less and less. Food banks now have to ration, as demand outstrips donations. One day a young mother at the drop-in was in despair. The food bank would not give her any milk for her child. You could only have milk if you had two or more children. At CANE we no longer get coffee for our meetings from Winnipeg Harvest. For four years we had been getting coffee. Now there is none available. The donations to all charities are getting less and less. In 1996 donations to the Sunshine Fund, the fund to send children to summer camp, dropped 30%.[51] Loran Fried, executive-director of North York Harvest Food Bank in Toronto said there was a 25% drop in donations to the food bank he runs. The reason for this may be donor burnout. But the reason he perceives is "cynicism about the poor."[52]

Who are "the poor." The poor are always "the other." The media, the politicians and the society as a whole have two interesting perceptions of "the poor." One is related to the cynicism Fried mentions. This is the attitude of negative judgment. The negative judgment is fed by two strands. One is that the poor are lazy and not trying hard enough to get a job. The other is that the poor are not "really" poor. They do not look poor. It is incredible, but true that the helpers think the helped should really be poor. We should be in rags and have no material possessions. I heard a woman talking about the beggars on the street. She was incensed that they were dressed so well. I heard another woman complain that the people she delivered Christmas hampers to had a big television set. It takes a long time for all our possessions to wear out and break down. The other perception of "the poor" is the helpless losers. I remember one of our members being outraged by seeing one of the television reporters smiling and sweetly saying how "We should all help the poor." This condescending attitude is soul-destroying.

If this is the stereotype of our fellow citizens living in poverty, it is no wonder that the relationship between giver and receiver is one of power and dependency. The professional helpers and those who volunteer time or money, either in public or private institutions, are the winners. Those at the bottom, the losers, gradually have less and less connection with those in the market economy. Finally there is no connection at all. The ideal in our society becomes the self-sufficient banker. In a Monty Python skit this ideal is played by John Cleese as the banker who is asked to give a pound to an orphanage. At first he thinks it is an investment opportunity or a tax dodge. The ideal of giving is incomprehensible.

> CLEESE: No? Well, I'm awfully sorry I don't under
> stand. Can you just explain exactly what you
> want.
> SOLICITOR: Well, I want you to give me a pound, and
> then I go away and give it to the orphans.
> CLEESE: Yes.
> SOLICITOR: Well, that's it.
> CLEESE No, no, no, I don't follow this at all. I mean, I

don't want to seem stupid but it looks to me as though I'm a pound down on the whole deal.

SOLICITOR: Well, yes you are.

CLEESE: I am! Well what is the incentive to give you the pound?

SOLICITOR: Well, the incentive is to make the orphans happy.

CLEESE: (genuinely puzzled) Happy? You're quite sure you've got this right?

Charity: Love or Judgment

We can laugh at the banker who is totally self-centered. We know that he does not represent the majority of Canadians. There still is in this country a real wish to help one's fellow citizens. We want to be charitable. We are just not sure how to go about it.

I have to be very careful what I say on this subject. I have discovered that if I say anything negative about charity or about organized "charities" I am considered ungrateful, or worse. One day I was talking with a CBC radio reporter. She was very proud of the work they were doing to raise money for Winnipeg Harvest, the Winnipeg food bank. I told her that our organization was considering picketing their Christmas breakfast program that raised money for Harvest. This would be to show that we did not want to live on charity. The reporter was highly insulted. She said that she would continue to do her "good work," because she was a Christian.

A Christian ideal has always been to be charitable. This ideal was based on Christian texts, most notably 1 Corinthians 13:3 "I may give away all that I have to the poor, and even give my body to be burned, but if I have not charity, I am nothing." But what does charity mean?

The word charity once referred to a particular relationship between people. The Greek word "agape" was first translated as charity, and then as love. Still today the dictionary gives the full meaning for the word charity. The word means "love towards one's self, and one's neighbour." But it is defined even more clearly than that. The love is non-judgmental. The dictionary says charity means "forbearance in judging others." If the word charity still meant non-judgmental love, then it would indeed be the highest ideal one could seek. Non-judgmental love does not mean power over someone. It means standing with your friend.

However, the dictionary has another meaning, and this is the one that everyone believes is the definition of charity. The literal meaning is given as "to help the poor." The dictionary does not say this, but the society that we live in considers charity as helping the poor in a particular way. Most people today think charity means alms-giving, that is giving money or physical things to those less fortunate than themselves.

Charity today encompasses everything from giving money to the beggar on the street to supporting the welfare state. CANE was written about in the Winnipeg Free Press. It quoted one of our members as saying she did not have a winter coat. The next day someone phoned CANE and offered a winter coat. Unfortunately it was the wrong size. In order for June to get a coat that fit, her welfare worker had to give her money. Her worker said no. We have found that there is no reason why some get money for winter coats, and some do not. When someone is lucky enough to actually get money for a coat, is the money welfare gives for a coat charity? Is charity only when a woman phones with an offer of a used coat? Is all giving charity? Is charity anything that one person gives to another, without it being money paid for work done?

Charity today is about alms-giving to those who do not work in the market economy. Those who do work in the market economy, and who receive money for this work, are the givers, and those who work in different ways are the receivers of charity. This view of the world is often expounded in the media. For example, Tom Oleson says that charity is always well meant, and welfare is charity - but long term dependency on charity inevitably erodes a person's feeling of worth.[53] He assumes that money received freely, instead of in exchange for work, is a bad thing. Our understanding of charity today is all wrapped up in that old work ethic. It has very little to do with the original meaning of agape, which is non-judgmental love given freely with no strings attached.

Today charitable giving to those at the bottom is about power and judgment. The giver of money is usually the morally righteous, respectable worker. This is not always true because people with very little can be very generous with the little they have. However, if you have to prove to someone both that you need money to live, and that you are worthy to receive this money, then the givers are the judges, those in control. The control can be obvious, or masked, but the receiver is well aware of it. In all cases the person who is giving the money has the power to say whether the receiver eats or goes hungry. It is clear that this type of charity is bondage or slavery.

Shifting Boundaries:

"A boundary is an artifact of our moral will"[54]

A) There is a boundary line between justice and charity, a line that shifts. The philosopher, Kant says that moral progress consists of the expansion of the realm of justice into what was previously the domain of charity.[55] In Canada the boundary between the charitable institution (constraint) and public, universal social programs (covenant) has shifted in the opposite direction. Marlene Webber subtitles her book "How our dollar democracy drove 2 million Canadians into food banks to collect private charity in place of public justice." The first indication of the shift can be pinpointed. In 1981 the first food bank opened in Canada. We now have more food banks than McDonald's restaurants. Our leaders have now shifted the boundary so that charity has expanded, and "the poor" are demonized, judged and controlled.

Our politicians actively encourage the shift from public to private. They are then praised by the media for their acts of private charity. One obvious example in Winnipeg is the praise given to Ron Duhamel, Liberal MP for St. Boniface. People are plunged into deeper poverty by the cutbacks in transfer payments legislated by Duhamel and his fellow Liberals. Duhamel's response is to have "charity drives for school supplies." For several years he has helped gather pencils, erasers and other school supplies for "needy, under privileged children." The media seem unable to connect the two actions.

With the 1996 federal budget the Liberals took $7 billion dollars out of transfer payments to the provinces. This money would have gone to health, education and welfare. Then all the provinces cut money out of these programs and blamed the federal government. The expectation was that the private sector would pick up the slack. People like Duhamel are held up as examples to follow. Unfortunately, the private sector is totally unable to make up what has been taken away. The Canadian Centre for Philanthropy has determined through its research that for every 1% reduction in government spending the charitable sector would need a 6% increase in donations from individuals, companies and foundations to make up the shortfall. Rather than increases we have seen donor burnout at all levels. Is it any wonder that the poor are getting poorer?

B) There has also been a radical shift within the welfare system itself. The boundary between justice and charity has shifted within the welfare system. The public welfare system now works on the charity model. The bonds of constraint are tightening. This shift took place after the 1996 federal budget. Not only were billions of dollars taken out of the system, but the rights that had been in place within the Canada Assistance Plan were not put into the new legislation. During the previous few years the provinces had been ignoring the legal rights of Canadians by implementing workfare and by lowering welfare rates to destitution levels. However, the federal government ignored these practices.

Once the rights were taken out of the legislation it was open season on the poor. In Manitoba the rates went down again. Single moms with children were re-classified as "employable." Disabled people were systematically denied provincial welfare and reclassified as "employable" so that they receive $70 dollars a month less. Then all the "employables" began to be channeled into job-finding clubs, and to be hounded night and day.

The welfare system has always been bureaucratic and paternalistic. Today it is a horror that people will do anything in their power to avoid. Not only have the rates been lowered to destitution level, people are hounded to utter despair. What makes it unspeakably unjust is that there are no rules within the system. It is totally arbitrary. One person gets a winter coat, and another does not. One person gets a bus pass to job-search and another does not. One person has to produce proof of twenty job applications a week and another does not.

C) The third boundary shift has been between the employed and the unemployed. Many Canadians used to receive a living wage for the work they did. This group has gotten smaller and smaller. The group of workers who do not fit this criteria is now one-third of the work force. Thousands of workers have part-time, contract, temporary work that does not give them an adequate income. Bruce O'Hara calls these workers "distressed workers." Besides the unemployed and part time workers this group includes under-employed, seasonal workers and my husband's favourite category "non-viably self-employed." As a playwright he, and the vast majority of the others in the artistic community, are "non-viably self-employed." Some people call these workers "non-standard workers." We decided to call ourselves non-employed.

Most workers refuse to identify themselves with any of the above categories. Workers with any kind of job for any period of time will call themselves employed. There have been people who refused to get involved with CANE because we called ourselves non-employed. It was too shameful to admit that you were not employed. The government also calls these workers employed. It certainly helps their unemployment statistics. The statistics do not realistically reflect the fact that the employed workforce is closer to 75%, rather than the 90% in the official statistics.

All these shifting boundaries have been the result of those in positions of power making deliberate decisions. We have chosen to expand the area of constraint, wrongly called charity. We have chosen to shape all our institutions to exclude as many people as possible, and then to judge those we have excluded. "We have made the poor into shame-faced children. Those who are denied access to a job at a living wage are viewed as deficient.

We can then mistreat them without guilt." [56]

3) BOND: UNITING FORCE

The lack of the covenant bond, and the refusal to accept the bond of restraint, has led some people to put all their energies into creating community. Within a community goods and services are shared. Everyone is included. It is assumed that everyone has something to offer, that is, everyone has a gift, whether money, skill, energy or just the willingness to participate. The structures that are built assume individual competence and collective action. The helping is always a two-way street, never assuming that one person is the one with power and the other is dependent. The wish to help others is reciprocal, and part of what it means to be human. The helping is an uniting force. "A sense of bondedness is at the heart of helping." [57]

It is a challenge to form community, especially if the people involved begin from very different situations. In Central America there are communities of voluntary and involuntary poor. They are called base communities, and are based on the ideas generated by liberation theology. Around the world there are communities whose purpose is to include people who have been excluded. Jean Vanier, a Canadian, has built L'Arche communities in many countries. These communities bring together those who have limited mental ability, and those who are considered "normal."

In Canada there are more and more examples of people coming together to create economic communities. Small groups of people join together, pool resources, and work to create economic resources for everyone. In some cases it is a deliberate attempt to challenge the idea of helping through what is now called "the charity model." An example in Winnipeg is the Christmas L.I.T.E. program. This campaign began when people decided to create an alternative to the traditional Christmas Cheer Board charity. Their pamphlet says "This initiative takes the concept of giving at Christmas beyond the charity model, addresses the root causes of poverty, and helps under-developed communities become self-sufficient." The program encourages those in Winnipeg who have money to share at Christmas to help their fellow citizens by buying locally from Native cooperatives. Their pamphlet says "give a family a hamper and you feed then for a few days. Contribute to the development of their community, and you give them the tools they need to feed themselves for a lifetime."

The Christmas L.I.T.E. program involves a small group of people in Winnipeg at Christmas time. Is it possible for the City of Winnipeg, or for Canada itself, to become united in common cause? We have seen larger communities, cities and provinces work together on a temporary basis. People help each other when there is a natural disaster. In Canada, in the last few years, there have been plenty of those. Floods and ice-storms have brought out a spirit of community. People from all walks of life join together. In Winnipeg thousands of volunteers built dikes, made sandwiches and did all the variety of tasks needed. All were united in a common cause. The people who needed help were not judged deserving or undeserving. Food and other supplies were given generously to all.

Then the flood is over, and life goes back to normal. For those of us living in poverty the flood is never over. After the waters went down, and most people went back into their homes, the people at CANE started to talk about what had happened. We had seen the community rally around to help those in trouble. Many of us wondered why the community does not rally around those who have no work. For those who are laid off, or who never find work, their life is a continuing disaster beyond their control. It is a disaster they face alone.

The question that we were really asking was: "Why does no one care about us?" We know that you do not really care for us when your care is expressed through dropping off a tin of soup into the Harvest bin. Your care will be expressed when you come and be with us, share in our community, share your time, or your money, or your energy. We know how hard that can be for our fellow Canadians. It might even demand a sacrifice. That is the one component to community that may also be necessary.

SECTION III:
We are the People; Listen to Us

In this ferocious era, if we are to keep ourselves human, and to be effective citizens, then our first obligation is to be free. And by free I mean knowing the truth about things, to know what is so, without simplifications, without false hopes, without moral fervour divorced from moral clarity.

GEORGE GRANT, *A Critique of the New Left*

I HAVE RECENTLY BECOME AWARE of a variation on the reporter's question "How do you feel about that?" Not only is the expected response "I feel bad," some media people have now decided that feeling bad assumes that one feels he or she is a victim. Being a victim is apparently not acceptable in some circles. John Colliston's 1290 Talk Radio phone-in show had called and asked if I would speak with Colliston on the radio. I agreed. After a long discussion, during which he made a number of negative comments about people living in poverty, a caller began to speak about victims. Colliston suddenly went on a tirade about people like me, that is, people who always blame others for their circumstances, and who think they are victims. He cut me off before I could explain that I was not a victim. In fact, I am a Canadian citizen who feels empowered and free.

For a long time I felt locked into a slavery of powerlessness, but no more. Unfortunately, many thousands of Canadians who live in poverty still accept negative feelings as inevitable.

They accept living in fear of others and of life; they accept the external judgment of others on who they are, and then live in guilt; they believe there are no choices, and then live in despair; or they live in a state of constant anger. This negative cycle of emotions keeps those marginalized in our society in a constant state of immobility, with flashes of ineffective lashing out at the powers that be.

There is an assumption that these negative feelings are beyond one's control, and that there is nothing that can be done. Our feelings somehow are external to ourselves and in the control of other people. Most of us have bought into Behaviourism, which maintains everything, including feelings are externally controlled. Other people work hard at attempting to control our feelings through emotional manipulation. The emotional carrot is some version of "pumping us up" through various job-finding clubs, and the emotional stick is bringing us down through a blaming, shaming welfare system.

This emotional manipulation does seem to work, and so the systems continue to use it. However, it does not work with everyone. The people that are engaged in the process are then puzzled, and try harder to make it work. No one questions the basic assumptions about how people work. Once we really look closely at how people work it becomes obvious that carrots and sticks only work if everyone believes the carrot is worth having. Someone might say, "I don't like carrots," or "I like carrots, but I am not prepared to do what you say in order to get one." People are like that. In the final analysis people decide whether they will struggle for the carrot or not. People are internally controlled.

Regardless of the fact that not everyone reacts as they are supposed to, those in positions of authority continue their quest to control our feelings and our behaviour. We are expected to spend all of our lives looking for paid work in the marketplace, regardless of the fact that there are not enough paid jobs at a living wage for everyone. We are expected to "market" ourselves. The other day one of the staff from a Winnipeg job-finding club came down to the CANE office to check us out. Her job is to "market the clients." Not only are we expected to market ourselves, if we cannot do the job others will be paid to help us in this endeavour. On top of this those people living on social assistance live at a destitution level with never enough for the basics of life. The modern day slave markets continue to work very effectively at enslaving people.

At this point every one of us who lives on the margins can make a choice. We can continue to feel powerless, and to play the victim role, or we can make an internal reality shift. It is possible to decide to be happy. On my wall at the CANE office I had a saying by Wendell Berry "Be joyful, even though you have considered all the facts." I have heard every reason why this is impossible. In fact I have argued for years with my husband that it is impossible to be happy in the situation we find ourselves in. I decided to write a book outlining how bad things were, and how bad we all feel. The most interesting thing happened. Setting it all down was in fact an important part of the process of healing. In particular, writing about anger was healing because that is the part of me that is most negative. So I wrote it all down, and then began to write the positive chapters. And I got stuck for a year. I could not make the internal reality shift. I could not decide to be happy.

During 1998 some important things happened that opened the real possibility of living a full and joyful life. The cycle of negative feelings had been operating most effectively because I felt so isolated. The positive circles of faith, forgiveness, hope and joy became possible when I became connected to two broader communities. The first instance was reconnecting to a Christian community for the first time in fifteen years. The second was making a connection with the labour movement. The Canadian Union of Postal Workers (CUPW) has opened a Workers Organizing Resource Centre (WORC). This is a pilot project in Winnipeg. They invited CANE and other community groups to share their office space, supplies and equipment for free.

At some level I felt a part of the broader community of people who struggle for justice. I continued to read the books of people who talk about alternative ways of living. There are only a few I have found who not only write about living life in a different way, but who actually live a full and joyful life with others in community. The writings of Jean Vanier and of Anne Schaef have been particularly helpful. Vanier has built communities of "normal" and mentally handicapped people all over the world. He saw an alternative to institutionalizing people and focusing on their lack and their sickness. Anne Schaef also, after many years involved in healing systems that focus on sickness, not health, began to search for a better way. She saw that all our institutions were sick or addictive and finally she turned to Aboriginal peoples for wisdom.

Reading about people who live in a place of peace and joy is different from actually living there oneself. However, the reading brings us closer and closer to the decision making. Gradually I saw more and more clearly. The major block I kept stumbling on was the idea that one lived in a positive way or a negative way. One lived in the light or in the dark. My struggle was always how to acknowledge the reality of the dark while living in the light. Could I allow myself to be happy knowing how destructive the society I live in is?

Finally I read something that enabled me to make the

decision, the internal shift, the decision that it was possible to live in the light. I read one of Herbert O'Driscoll's books. He said that a human life is like the floor of a forest. There is light and darkness everywhere. The forest is a single living form where the two mingle together. We all need the light, not flashes of light now and then, but a constant source of steady light. The grace of God can be like that.

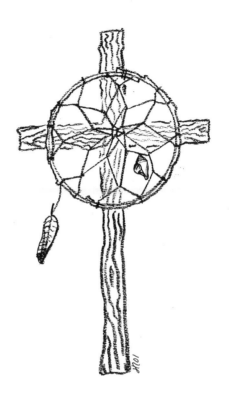

Chapter Nine:
THE TRUTH SHALL MAKE YOU FREE

Humanity continues on a journey that is both beautiful and disastrous. But I believe that the universe and humanity have been well made, that they contain within them elements of balance and healing.

JEAN VANIER, *Our Journey Home*

Living a life of faith is not passive or lazy. It is doing the best we can, and then letting go.

ANNE SCHAEF, *Meditations for People who Worry too Much*

WE COULD EASILY HAVE TAKEN MORE PEOPLE to St. Charles Retreat Centre. Sister Olive is flexible in how much she will charge us. She would have accepted a few more. We had phoned approximately one hundred people, but only eight signed up to go. Robert, my husband, was leading the retreat, so we had nine people, a good-sized group for group discussion. But I wondered why more did not want to come. I brought the issue up at the CANE Steering Committee. I said that I was trying to figure out why more people would not want to go to a place where they had a room and good food in a beautiful spot. They would be going with friends. The answer from the Steering Committee was that it was too scary to lay down the burden of our life for even a day. Sally said that middle class people go to the cottage and relax for a weekend. They give themselves permission to do this. They know that they will take up their work, their struggles, their burdens whether light or heavy on Monday. But on the weekend they can relax. For those of us living on the edge there is no possibility of laying down the burden of our lives for even a day. I said that I remembered a woman at one of our Tuesday meetings who job searched every day and never stopped. The group said that it is not only the job search. It is the fear of not having enough to eat. So the non-employed have to keep struggling in fear. There is no time for rest or a retreat. I thought then what incredible courage it takes to entertain the possibility that life can be more than just endured, and that the fear can be laid aside.

So the nine brave souls had set out for the day at St. Charles in high hopes, and now we were sitting on the deck waiting for the bus home. The deck overlooks the Assiniboine River. Below us was only the river and the trees. It was a beautiful summer evening. We talked about what we had learned in the last twenty-four hours, and what a good time it had been. We had begun on the evening that we arrived by talking about what we expected from our time here, what we wanted to learn, and what, if any, religious experiences we had had. We learned a lot about each other. Everyone felt free to share his or her story. Then it was time to go to our rooms. We stopped at the library to get books and magazines and paper and pens so that people could read or write if they did not want to sleep immediately.

The next day we continued to learn and to share in an atmosphere of peace and openness. It had been a healing experience. Now it was time to leave. Someone started to talk about what a good sleep he had had. As we talked some said that at home they often could not get to sleep until late, but here they had found that they could relax and have a good sleep. As I reflected on this I realized they had been given permission to leave their burdens at the door. They had been given permission to let go of the fear for a day. They could sleep deeply and well in a safe place, a place of peace.

Letting Go of Fear

A few people had let go of their fear for a day. Is it possible for us all to let go of our fear every day? The answer is yes. The process is as easy as snapping your fingers, and as hard as changing everything.

This is the second time in my life that I have struggled in the darkness, in fear and confusion, and then have finally, it seems miraculously, arrived at a place of clarity. The first time the struggle was to know how to create a loving family, to understand my children and to live in harmony with them. At the end of seven years of searching, when Robert and I felt confident enough to share our journey, we wrote *The Family Zoo*. When I once again found myself living in fear, and in a dark, threatening, confusing place I went back to the answers and the process that had evolved in our search for family harmony.

At first I did not even see the connections between my struggles in my family, and my struggles as a marginalized Canadian living in poverty. Gradually I identified the key question in both situations, and it is the same question. "How do I survive?" We experience the negative emotions as crippling and we wonder how we can survive emotionally. Both the parent who struggles to deal with a child who is having serious difficulties, and the person living in poverty, is trapped in fear and struggles desperately to survive emotionally. The only way to survive emotionally is to let go of fear and to live in faith, and that seems like an impossibility.

We are enslaved by fear. George Grant tells us that in order to be fully human and to be effective citizens we need to

be free. Fear binds us as surely as chains or ropes. The powers
that be do not need to be afraid of any challenge to the present
system because we are tightly bound by fear. I have talked with
community workers who say that people they know are even
afraid to vote. Our oppressors have done such an amazing job of
binding people so tightly in fear that there is no voice of resistance. Fear and all the companion negative emotions take up an
immense amount of energy. There is none left over to confront
our oppressors or to actively be involved in constructive changes.

      People not only do not seek to let go of their fear, there
is actually resistance to even considering letting go. On the
surface this does not make sense. If the fear is so crippling emotionally, then why can't we let it go? We cannot let it go because
we believe that if we do "they" have won. Letting go is seen as
the same as giving up. There is a resistance to the idea of becoming compliant, and of accepting a horrible situation. We
have this view of life that as long as there is injustice and pain
and suffering to me, or to anyone else in the world, then everyone has to remain miserable. The outcome of such a belief is
that those who oppress us not only control our bodies, they
control our souls.

The Change Process

Fear is an emotional response to the pictures we have in our
mind of the world we live in. But the pictures can change. The
result of this change is that the emotional responses change.
Robert and I often saw this change occuring when we taught
parenting courses. Parents would come in, sit down and outline
their reality. Their kids were bad and they were no good as
parents; life was a misery of fear, depression, anger; and there
was nothing they could do about it. We would acknowledge
that that was how they saw the world. Then we suggested that

we could view the world, and their families, in a different way.

In order to show that people can view the same situation in different ways we would bring out the old picture that everyone uses to show how the same picture can look like a vase or two faces. Everyone could see that. Then we would show a picture that could either be a young women in her twenties, or an old women in her eighties, depending how you looked at it. We asked the parent if they saw an old or a young woman. Then we showed them that there was another very different woman in the same picture. This was harder for people to see. We heard about one group where the people could not see the two faces, so they all compromised and said that the woman was middle aged. Sometimes people would pretend that they could see the different face because this was what they were supposed to do. We could always tell if this was what they were doing. There was no obvious change in them. There was no "Aha!" As more and more of the group saw the other picture there was great excitement and all the participants tried to help everyone else see the other picture. Reality was changed in the twinkling of an eye.

1) Changing Modalities

I have a picture in my head. We are all sitting around the big table at Crossways discussing a new project. There is a person at the meeting who is making life difficult for me. Her ideas and values are opposed to mine. I think that life is hard enough. I do not want to have to deal with her. I think that I should not have to deal with her. I get angry and resentful. Not only do I get angry because of what she is saying today. I become afraid of what she will say or do in the future. My brain is working very hard at creating a picture for me. This picture contains my perception of the person and my beliefs about the person. The final stage is to create all the negative feelings that accompany the picture.

My brain has done all this with the best of intentions, but I really do not want to stay in this reality. So I think that I will follow Richard Bandler's advice.[58] He points out that the pictures that we create in our brains are rich and complex. We experience the world through a multitude of senses. There is more than what I see. We tend to lay great store in what we see. We even say "seeing is believing." But there is also sound, taste, touch, smell. There are also other modalities or modes of perception such as size and distance. All of these modalities can be changed.

I am now sitting at my dining room table at home and expressing my frustration. I am afraid that this person will cause trouble for me and for CANE. Robert comes over and asks me what I am afraid of. I say that I am afraid a certain person is going to make things difficult and cause disruption in CANE. He asks how big the person seems to me. I say that she seems large and threatening. So he tells me to make her small, which I do in my mind. We then add Mickey Mouse ears and circus music to the picture. Bingo - no more fear. It is ridiculously simple, but it works. When I see this person again there is no more fear. Not only that, I can deal with the situation assertively and competently.

A friend had a picture from the past that was still bothering her. So we added Mickey Mouse ears to the person who had put down my friend, and the person started to talk in a Mickey Mouse voice. There are hundreds of ways that we can use our brain to change the sights, sounds, touch, smell, taste, size of the past, and of the future. We can also disassociate from frightening experiences by looking at the experience from a distance. The experience is put on a movie screen and we then sit and watch it. We can also be in the projection booth and run

---

the movie fast or slow, or backwards. Our minds are incredibly creative when we permit them to be. Alone or with a friend's help we can change modalities until the fear, or any other negative emotion is gone.

We all have these fearful pictures in our minds. Some become so intense that they become phobias. Someone may look at a mouse and become paralyzed with fear. Some of us may look at the welfare office, or the clerk in the welfare office, and become paralyzed with fear. Any previous bad experience can trigger a fear response, but all these responses can be changed by changing modalities.

Changing modalities is a learned skill. Anyone can do it and the more you do it the easier it becomes. There are many books by Bandler and other people available in bookstores and libraries. After a while the skill becomes automatic, and we can do it without thinking. It is like learning to drive a car. At first it is difficult, but soon it is automatic.

The question is "Do you want to do it?" Robert and I were watching the National Film Board video "Democracy a la Maude." There were numerous shots of Conrad Black putting down Maude Barlow and her supporters from the Council of Canadians. At the end we said, "That was incredible! Conrad Black walks with a swagger and talks with a sneer." We collapsed in laughter. Now in our family mentioning Conrad Black brings hilarity instead of fear. He is still doing the same mean things, but he has no control over me and how I feel. I am not tied up in helpless rage when I see him. It feels more like laughter and pity.

When we decided to watch the video about Maude Barlow it was a wish to focus on the positive. We discovered that Conrad Black was a large part of the program. However, at the end we were left with a positive feeling about how one person uses her gifts, talents and energy to create an alternative vision for Canada and for Canadians. In this video we have two powerful people and we can decide which one to focus on. The problem is that in most of our lives there are far more negative people and events than positive ones. However, the decision is the same decision. If there is only one positive event that happened this month, or even this year, regardless of what else happened, we can still choose to focus our attention and our memory on that one event.

One day my daughter Elizabeth was looking for a certain skirt. She looked all over and could not find it. It had just come out of the wash and was still wet. Elizabeth was very upset. Then she stopped and said "OK that's what I can't do. What can I do?"

Sometimes it is obvious what we should focus on and other times it is not. If we feel that there is nothing good anywhere the answer is usually to expand our focus, to look at the big picture. We can do this by expanding our time focus or our space focus.

Most people in our society have a very short attention span. People like the Nisga'a in BC are capable of demanding their rights for one hundred years until a treaty is finally signed. When we are talking about social change the time lines are usually pretty long. I remember once reading about the churches in the United States trying to decide whether slavery was right or wrong. Some thought it was right, and some thought it was wrong, and some thought it was each person's personal decision. The discussion continued at all levels for fifty years before the major churches in the United States decided slavery was wrong.

Just as our time focus is usually pretty short, our space focus is usually pretty small. Our focus tends to be on ourselves, and what is happening to us. If our lives seem filled with problems, we tend to think that it is all our fault and that we are no good. One day during a discussion at CANE we were talking about having faith in ourselves. Once again people reminded each other "Don't take it personally." All the oppressive systems are not set up to get me. They are set up to control everyone. The larger focus frees us from a small confined place of darkness.

This shift of focus is not saying that the bad things do not happen. This is not saying that the bad things should be ignored. This is saying that I choose to live in the light rather than in the darkness. By making this choice I am also making the world a lighter place for all those around me.

2) Changing Models

All the pictures in our mind are like the bits and pieces of a puzzle. They need to be fitted together. Our wondrous brain takes all the bits and pieces and puts them together into a whole, into a model of reality. This is especially hard to do in our society. We live in the "Information Age." This does not mean that we have knowledge or wisdom. It means only that the number of disconnected, irrelevant facts is expanding exponentially. Unfortunately, at the same time, important facts are left out or contradict each other. Too often the result is confusion, not clarity.

Regardless of the overwhelming number of bits and pieces of the puzzle, that may or may not fit, people have a real need to make sense of the world. Everyone continues to fit everything together into their reality. People then assume that the way they put the bits and pieces together is the correct way. Someone else's interpretation of reality may be different from mine, but I assume my model is "reality." This is a statement of belief. My reality, my model, is the true one.

Where do our models come from? We learn our models from all the authorities in our lives. First our parents, then the school system and, from an earlier and earlier age, television. The pictures that we carry around in our heads are not just the pictures from the lives we lead. We are also bombarded night and day by other pictures coming into our living rooms. Sometimes the pictures and sounds from the box become more real than those from our lives. Here is a reality that someone else has deliberately created for us. It is a reality where news, situation comedy, movies and commercials are so similar that fiction and non-fiction are part of the same reality. Sometimes when I watch *This Hour has 22 Minutes* I am not sure what is part of the show and what is a commercial.

Noam Chomsky explains how our models are made. He shows how models are built. We take all the bits and pieces, and then the process of deletion, distortion and generalization occurs. People's minds just delete what does not fit. Arnold Palmer, the golfer, was being interviewed. The interviewer asked him how he coped when he "shanked" the ball. (Do not ask me what "shanked" means. I assume it is a bad thing.) Palmer said "Oh, I never shank the ball." The interviewer said "Oh yes. I saw you do that at Pebble Beach last month." Palmer said "I don't remember." He did not remember. He just deleted the memory. Shanking the ball did not fit with the image he had of himself.

Everyone distorts what they see and hear in order to fit their model. How many times have you repeated a conversation and put in a little twist just to make yourself look better, or to prove a point that you want to make. Finally, what is most obvious is generalizations. Generalizations about groups of people are constantly repeated. If you think all politicians are crooks, then no matter what a politician does it will be interpreted as crooked. I used to shake up people when they said "All politicians are crooks." I would say "My husband is a politician, and he is not a crook." This would stop them in their tracks. There would be a desperate struggle to fit this fact into the model. Finally, the response would be "Oh, I don't mean your husband." This response allowed them to keep their model in tact.

Even when people are forced to beg in the street, or to get food at a food bank, they keep their model intact. One of the scenes in Patrick Watson's documentary on democracy shows a man being interviewed. He, with his wife and children, live in a car under a bridge. He says to the interviewer "America is the best country in the world." The fact that some people have no homes or no food, even the experience that I have no home or no food does not change one's model. If we believe that America, or Canada, is the best country in the world, no fact or statistic or experience will change this.

What will change our models? First the old model has to be seen to be incompatible with the values we hold. For example, our main value may be people. Our economic model does not take people, or the environment, into account. Therefore, we are forced to delete all the repercussions of the economic model on people and the environment. In effect, we force our mind to "dumb down." This is not hard when most of our information comes from the idiot box, but, there comes a day and a time when too many pieces do not fit. Maybe someone we trust points this out, or maybe we see something new. It is the last straw.

If we finally say that the old models are untenable, then we need to build up new ones. Fortunately, there are people who are thinking about, and writing about, new models. In some cases the new ways of living have developed communities of people committed to these new ways. There is L'Arche founded by Jean

Vanier. Anne Schaef has a world wide community based on the Living Process. Iyanla Vanzant has the Spiritual Life Maintance Network. In *The Reinvention of Work* Matthew Fox outlines a paradigm shift by contrasting the Machine Era with the Green Era.

No one clear alternative has yet been articulated for the society, but some parameters are becoming clearer. The new models are built on harmony, not control. When we live our lives in fear we have to control everything around us. Worry and fear are not part of the new models. What is common in all the new models or paradigms of reality is a vision of harmony within and between all peoples and the earth. The new models are built on an assumption of faith in ourselves, in others and in a higher power that is trustworthy.

LIVING IN FAITH

a) Faith in Myself

I can only have faith in myself when I truly know who I am, that is when I discover my identity. When I consider who I am, I begin with my birthday. I was born into this world on June 24th, St. Jean Baptiste Day. I have always identified with "a voice crying in the wilderness." Then I look at my family and community. My Métis great grandmother hid Louis Riel in her basement dressed in women's clothes in order to escape the authorities. My great-grandfather owned the Red Saloon on the corner of Portage and Main. There is no doubt that I am from Winnipeg. As a teenager one of the pivotal events in my life was listening to Tommy Douglas at the Winnipeg Auditorium. Thus, my model of economic and social reality was built on the social gospel movement.

There is a Maori saying "This is my place to stand." Anne

Schaef reflects on this. She says "my place to stand" means that I belong. I have a tribe. I have a land. Because of these connections my feet are rooted firmly in the earth of my ancestors and I have my place. I am not confused about who and what I am. I know. The Maori have observed that the white people seem ungrounded. They have no place to stand because they have no connection with their ancestors.[59]

We are not only a part of our personal and ancestral past. We are also unique. Each one of us has gifts, talents, something to offer, something that we should celebrate. One of my favourite stories about someone finding and using his gift is in Mary Schramm's *Gifts of Grace*. A middle-aged engineer was part of an inner-city congregation in Washington, D.C. The congregation was determined to minister to the area, and to use the gifts of each member. Bob decided that his gift was building model airplanes. The rest of the group were not impressed, and suggested other possible gifts, but he insisted that was his gift. A few days later the minister was talking to a playground supervisor in the area. The supervisor said that he had eight boys who really needed help. They were interested in taking part in a model airplane contest. He asked the minister if he knew of anyone who could help.

Finally, who we are is manifest in what we do. We find a harmony between who we are and the actions we take. We take our identity from our heritage and our gifts and we find the unique work that we are called to do. We may know what this work is when we are very young. Some of us may take a lifetime to find it. Part of the new model is that it is the process, not the end result, that gives our life meaning.

The issue of work and identity is key. According to a 1995 Maclean's magazine poll 74% of respondents said that a big part of the way they view themselves revolves around the work they do. The work we do is defined as paid work in a market economy. This means that those of us without paid work are constantly struggling to prove that we are people of value. On the other hand many who have paid work in this new globalized economy find ourselves with McJobs such as telemarketing. I know that some people are quite happy doing this job. I once did it for two days and nearly went crazy. For me to have to do that job every day would be soul destroying. Matthew Fox asks "How many of us find satisfaction, not a crushing defeat of the spirit, in our workday existence?"

It is not only people who have no paid work, or who have jobs that do not pay a living wage who struggle with their identity. People working at well-paid jobs in any of the helping professions also struggle with who they are. I listened to Eugenia Moreno, the Executive Director of the Canadian Association of Social Workers speak.[60] She had just been in Atlantic Canada and spoke of encountering social workers there who lacked confidence that their work could make a difference. Not only there, but all over Canada social workers see the social safety net being ripped apart and struggle to know how to respond. Moreno comes from Chile. She said that the social work profession there was split in two. The changes by the Chilean government were so destructive to people that social workers had to decide whether to be agents of social change or social control. Fear of losing one's job keeps many people from being agents of social change.

One of the turning points in my struggle to define the meaning of my life came the day I realized that if I died today I wanted to say that my life was more than a constant struggle to find work in the market economy. My life has meaning when everything I do is in harmony with my values. This means I spend time and energy clarifying my values, discovering my gifts, and seeking harmony within myself, with others and with God. It is a life's work, but what else should we do with our lives?

b) Faith in Others

One day I was at a party and began talking to a woman I had never met before. I told her that I was Chairperson of CANE, and we started to talk about unemployment. She began to tell me about her theories, and her solutions to the problem. She explained that all civil servants should get only a year contract, and then be replaced. I was ready to write her off, but I stopped and reminded myself that I should listen to her and try to understand her underlying concerns. So I began to question why she thought this would be a good solution. She started to talk about her experiences being unemployed. She felt people did not understand how terrible it felt. If everyone could experience a time of unemployment, then people would be more sympathetic to the unemployed, and would do more to help them. Her goal was to make sure that people would know what it felt like to be unemployed. Her way of reaching this goal did not make sense to me, but I discovered that her motives were good.

The usual response to a stranger at a party who seems to be blaming the unemployed and government workers would be to run away, or at least to quickly excuse yourself and seek more friendly company. We would then leave the party with another story about how mean people are, and our fear of others would be reenforced again. If , on the other hand, we begin with the premise that everyone is doing the best they can, and that we can have faith in people regardless of their misinformation, then another outcome is possible. Having faith in others is much more difficult, but it is possible. The first step is listening. From our years of teaching parenting classes I know that everyone believes in listening. Everyone believes that the other person should listen to them. The question posed by parents was always "How do I get my child to listen to me?" The question that actually will bring healing to the relationship is always "How do I listen to my child?" How do we listen to the other person? The skill of listening can be learned. It takes faith in the other person. Then it requires a patient search for the places where we agree and for the common goals we share, and it takes time. We constantly struggle with the issue of time. I once spent over an hour with an acquaintance who began by questioning me on why I did not have a job. At the end of the hour the acquaintance was a friend. Both of us were willing to take the time, and to get past the initial mistrust and negative feelings that were present at the beginning of the conversation. Unless we have faith in the other person we will not be willing to take the time.

Sometimes I wonder if there is a way for myself, and for others, to resurrect the value of taking the time to listen. It is not that we do not believe that listening is important. It is that so many other things are believed to be more important. Those who have no paid work spend all their time seeking work. Those who have work spend all their time working. Both need time to look after all life's daily needs. It is actually amazing that some people add seeking justice to their list of activities. How dedicated these people are, and how much time they spend in serving the broader community. I do not always agree with the tactics and strategy of others with similar goals and values to mine. Unfortunately, I do not take the time to know them, to understand why they do the things that they do. But I have faith that they are all doing the best they can for goals that we share.

c) Faith in God

I have often hesitated in bringing up the subject of God and spirituality. I did not want to be seen as someone forcing religion onto anyone else. However, I have found that when the subject comes up, the people at CANE are often very clear about the fact that it is only the grace of God that has kept them going. It seems that I am more hesitant than they are about raising the issue, but more and more I see how important it is in the lives of so many people, whether those people are involved in any particular church community or not.

Once we start talking about God or a Higher Power it is inevitable that the question is raised of how a loving God can allow such suffering. We know that everyone experiences both joy and sorrow, and everyone takes those experiences and tries to make sense of it all. The most helpful comment I have ever heard on this was given by my minister, David Widdicombe, one Sunday. He said that we can go through it all, the best and the worst, and we can do it with God or without God.

There are many different ways of living a spiritual life, and of having faith in oneself, in others, and in living a life of harmony with all people and with the earth. Gandhi led a revolution based on ahimsa, or non-violence towards all things. Thomas Merton said ahimsa (non-violence) is for Gandhi the basic law of our being. That is why it can be used as the most effective principle for social action, since it is in deep accord with the truth of our nature, and corresponds to our innate desire for peace, justice, order, freedom and personal dignity.

The Christian gospel can also be used in the same way. Around the world over many years there have been many who have led the way to peace and justice based on their Christian beliefs. There was Wilberforce in England who stopped the British slave trade; there was Martin Luther King Jr. in the United States; there was the whole social gospel movement in Canada led by people such as J.S. Woodsworth and Tommy Douglas.

The greatest social change in the last decade came about because of people such as Nelson Mandela and Bishop Desmond Tutu in South Africa whose lives are rooted in the Christian gospel. The media do not present the Christian base that sustains such people, nor the importance of the Christian values that prevented bloodshed in the struggle. I know the following story is recorded in a number of places, but I first heard it in a sermon that went like this:

"It happened during the weeks leading up to the multi-racial South African elections, when the great concern was over whether the Inkatha Freedom Party would participate. With all the violence that had been exchanged between supporters of Inkatha and supporters of the African National Congress, the fear was that if Inkatha did not come in, not only would the election lose some of its legitimacy, but that those going to the polls in the Inkatha stronghold of Natal would be clearly marked as supporters of the ANC, and that could lead to great bloodshed.

Feverish negotiations over participation went on for months and eventually an international effort was made to bring Inkatha in. Henry Kissinnger and Lord Carrington and a Kenyan diplomat unknown to the western media flew to South Africa to meet with Chief Buthelezi and his senior people. It was a day full of events, conferences, luncheons, arm-twisting behind the scenes, but there was no resolution. Finally, Dr. Kissinger held a press conference, saying no agreement had been reached and the situation was hopeless. With that, he got on his plane and flew back to the United States, as did Carrington to England. That much was reported by the media.

The Kenyan diplomat was not yet quite ready to give up. He followed the Buthelezi entourage to a smaller airport outside of Johannesburg only to find that the chief had already taken off for Natal. But, by chance, or by God, the plane developed engine trouble and had to return to the airport. And the diplomat got his second opportunity. He spoke again to the chief and said: "Chief Buthelezi, you are a Christian. Nelson Mandela is a Christian. I am a Christian. And in God's name, it is not right that Christians should be killing each other like this."

A few minutes later the plane took off a second time. And a couple of days later, the Inkatha Freedom Party caught everyone off guard by abruptly entering the electoral process. The encounter between Buthelezi and the unnamed Kenyan diplomat went unreported in the media. Well, the media would not know what to do with such a story." [61]

The True Self

Freedom is finally knowing and claiming your true self. That true self is a self filled with light, not darkness. Nelson Mandela has said "We were born to manifest the glory of God that is within us. It's not just in some of us, it's in everyone. And, as we let our own light shine, we consciously give other people permission to do the same. As we are liberated from our fear, our presence automatically liberates others." [62] This journey to discover our true self is a shared journey. "With us move millions of others, our companions in awakening from fear." [63]

The liberation comes from changing our perceptions of external reality. This change becomes possible when we step out in faith. I have faith in myself. I have faith in my gifts and talents no matter what any external person or organization says. I remember those times when I have used my gifts. I have occasionally run for public office. This is a scary thing to do. You are highly visible in your community, and everything you say is scrutinized. During a campaign the most highly charged, emotional events take place during public debates. One day I found myself in a school auditorium in St. James. There were five of us running for the School Board. We were on the stage sitting in front of a long table. In front of us were rows and rows of concerned people who had come out to hear our views of education. I looked out at the hundreds of people. I looked at my opponents, highly competent people, and I had a moment of panic. What was I doing here? I then realized that I knew all the issues, I had clear, well thought out positions, and I had years of experience standing before people and teaching them in the parenting classes Robert and I had led. I got up with a sense of knowing who I was, knowing I had the ability to teach. I had a feeling of joy and of the sense of my power. I enjoyed every minute of the evening.

I have decided to have faith in others precisely because I have seen that so many people have only conditional faith. How many times have we heard "She/he has to earn my trust." If external actions are the basis of our faith in others, no one will measure up. The world will be filled with darkness. I first learned the importance of having faith in others as I struggled to create a harmonious family. Even when our children had problems faith in them was essential regardless of their actions. Now, years later our children are the joy of our lives.

I have also seen the power of faith in my church community. When one of our members passed another step on the way to ordination, a number of people spoke about the beginning of the process. They laughed as they recounted that some of them had not been sure about his calling, but the group decided they would have faith in him. They now were rejoicing in how much he had learned and grown in every way over the last number of years.

To my delight I recently discovered a poem that expresses this struggle towards faith in others.

The hardest part is people.
So Lord, help me face them
without rancor of disappointment.
Help me see the pain behind their actions
rather than the malice;
the suffering rather than the rage.

Remind me...
That each time I close my heart
to another, I add to the darkness. [64]

I cannot go through life without considering faith in God. Faith in myself and in others is not a strong enough base for my life. I know there will be times when I add to the darkness, when other people hurt me and themselves. I know that sometimes when I least expect it, I am once again asking the questions - What is the meaning of life? Do I believe in a loving God? There is no easy way to explain how and why such moments come to us. I believe they come to everyone. Each one of us has a profoundly important story to tell about that encounter. Sometimes we are faced with a decision. We are totally responsible and capable of making such a decision. Sometimes it is elaborately set up so that the decision is clearly and forcefully set before us. But sometimes we are just wandering around aimlessly, doing our best, and we know that we have an opportunity to say Yes. When we say Yes, like John Wesley, the founder of Methodism, our hearts are "strangely warmed." At that moment all fear is driven out. We are truly free.

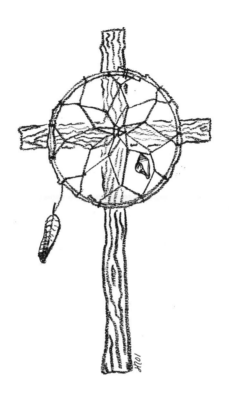

CHAPTER 10

COMMUNITY: LOVE IS THE PRACTICE OF FREEDOM

I have decided to stick with love.
Hate is too great a burden to bear.
MARTIN LUTHER KING JR.,
CHRISTMAS SERMON ON PEACE

I believe that it is in choosing love and beginning with love as
the ethical foundation for politics, that we are best positioned
to transform society in ways that enhance the collective good
. . . To choose love is to choose to live in community.
BELLE HOOKS, *Teaching to Transgress*

W
HEN I WAS IN UNIVERSITY IN THE 1960s there were great
discussions about social justice and changing society
for the better. We all thought it could be done, and
we would be the people to do it. And to a certain extent this
was true. It was in the 1960s in Canada that our last major
federal/provincial social programs, the Canada Assistance Act and
Medicare, were put into place. I, and many other students,
were part of the large group of people from all segments of
society that demanded these programs. We lobbied and marched
until we got them. It was an exciting time.

The political struggle was where the action was, and there
was very little talk about love or community building. How-

ever, there was one group at the university that had a commitment to justice, but also to community. This was the Student Christian Movement. Every summer I would attend an SCM work camp. Each camp would have a theme. During my first summer in Toronto I was at the Industrial Work Camp and a Mental Health work camp. This meant that we worked in factories during the day. At night we studied labour issues and how to build community. Part of being a community meant sharing resources including money. We not only discussed sharing everything, we did it. We had a wage pool where wages were shared at the end of the summer according to need. We had a travel pool, so that the people from Toronto and Vancouver and Halifax all paid the same to come to the camp.

We shared because we were a part of a community. We believed in sharing because most of us came from a Christian background. However, none of us had ever really shared like this before, or even knew that such a thing was possible. What if everyone believed in sharing? What if it was possible to build a society where everyone had enough? I did not know it at the time, but these radical ideas had been around for a long time in Canada. The SCM was part of a substantial minority within the Canadian Christian church. This group of people responded to the crisis of the great depression of the 1930s by forming the Fellowship for a Christian Social Order. They believed that the response to the crisis of world depression was to be based on the conviction that God is love and that love is mutuality or solidarity. This movement was called the social gospel movement.

I had heard about the social gospel movement, but knew very little about it. Then one day on the Winnipeg Public Library discard table I found a book called *Towards the Christian Revolution*. It was a republication of a book written in 1936 by a group of eminent Canadian theologians, economists and historians. They believed that the faith of the prophets and of Jesus was a "disturbing renovating force," and such a revolutionary teaching was what was needed as a response to the crisis we faced. This new edition was published in 1989 with a new introduction. It was published in the hope that their ideas had something to say in the current time of crisis. But in 1989 we did not yet believe that we were in crisis. The book languished in the library and finally made it to the discard table. What was trash to everyone else has become a treasure to me. My history, and Canada's history contains treasure.

In the 1930s people had come together in order to condemn greed, to abolish exploitation of their fellow human beings and to do this through non-violence. The beginning of this movement was a new organization called the Movement for a Christian Social Order. The statement of belief called for "the subordination of institutions to human need, the condemnation of acquisitiveness and the socialization of the agencies of production." The organization was founded in 1931. By 1934 there was an additional component. People felt the need to have fellowship among Christians who had become Christian socialists and the Fellowship for a Christian Social Order was formed. It became a nation-wide, non-denominational organization with local units in every province of Canada. This group, like the SCM in the universities, spent a lot of time in study groups. They not only studied together, they worshiped together and sang together. Song books were created. Has there ever been a social movement without music? They saw an integral connection between personal growth, ritual, social analysis and social justice activities.

It is not surprising that the leaders of the social gospel movement were also founding members of the League for Social Reconstruction, which became the CCF, which became the NDP. And Canada was set on the path of Hospitalization, Medicare, Old Age Pensions, Unemployment Insurance, and social assistance. Then came the war, and then came prosperity. Then came the culture of contentment. Many of us lived in the Canadian middle class, and life was good.

Life was good for white North Americans. In the 1960s work camps the SCM was still discussing sharing resources, but we had a lot of resources to share. Our fellow students in the United States were preoccupied with more drastic concerns. There was the war in Vietnam and the civil rights movement. Here was a new movement where black and white, students, workers and professionals joined together in a struggle against racism. For many in the struggle the reason for their involvement was a new understanding of their Christian faith. Many in the struggle, when attacked and tortured and imprisoned, drew strength from their faith. A black, activist, feminist writer who has taken the name Belle Hooks, writes about the civil rights movement. She says that the civil rights movement transformed society in the United States because it was fundamentally rooted in a love ethic, including love of one's enemies.[65] (It can be viewed that Malcolm X and the Black Power movement were concerned more with black self-love. She says that tragically the leaders of both movements were killed before their visions were fully integrated.)

When reflecting on the situation today hooks says that there is no powerful discourse on love emerging from politically progressive radicals or from the Left. She maintains that we must collectively return to a radical political vision of social change rooted in a love ethic. She sees this as the alternative to the culture of domination which is fundamentally anti-love and requires violence to sustain it. To choose love is to go against

---

the prevailing values of the culture. To choose love is to choose community.

Belonging

When we are part of a community we belong. The need to belong is inherent in all of us. It used to be clear where one belonged. Each one of us used to belong to a family, a neighbourhood, a community, a country. When I grew up on Strathcona Street in the West End of Winnipeg in the 1950s the neighbourhood was my community. Within walking distance there was my school, my community club, my church, even my extended family.

The cult of rugged individualism has created a society of isolated individuals who no longer belong anywhere. However, there still needs to be a mechanism for people to interact, and for a society to work. Unfortunately, most interactions today are not within communities. Most people interact within huge bureaucratic institutions. Even the interactions within the bureaucracies now, more and more, take place between people and machines. The Nellie McClung Theatre Group has a wonderful sketch where a man with an excruciating headache tries to get medical attention. He receives a recorded message when he dials a medical office. He has to keep punching numbers related to his symptoms until he finally falls over and dies. The machine is still asking him to punch in the next appropriate number.

When people receive assistance from recorded messages they may get some of their needs met. At least physical needs are usually partially met. But the needs for meaning and love and community are not even considered significant. We have created a "society of strangers." Michael Ignatiaff, in his book *The Needs of Strangers*, asks "What do humans need to be human?"

He lists the need for love, respect, honour, dignity and solidarity with others as the needs that have to be met so that human beings may flourish, not just survive. He maintains that these human needs are no longer considered part of political action; that such spiritual needs have passed into silence.

And yet the need to belong is so strong within us that it pops up when we least expect it, in unexpected places. The most interesting example for me is the Reform Party which swept to amazing popularity with the slogan "The West Wants In." They tapped into people's wish to belong to Canada, and not be excluded from the decision making of the country. For only the people who belong to the community can make the decisions for the community.

The issue of who belongs to what community has created incredible problems in the search for building a cohesive Canadian society. Who is in and who is out and who has the power to do what fuels French/English, Aboriginal/Non-Aboriginal, Federal/Provincial political clashes. Most of these issues are power issues and money issues. Who has the money to do what? In all these cases groups are fighting groups within the larger community. However, something more devastating is happening to Canadian society. Individuals are being pushed out of what for many is their most important community, their work community, and have no resources to belong to any other communities. Thousands of people are being marginalized. We are beginning to witness the breakdown of social cohesion.

At the time when individual needs for belonging are discounted, there is beginning to be recognition of the need for social cohesion in order for a country to be healthy. Someone, somewhere, in the Senate of Canada recognized this trend towards lack of social cohesion and the Senate Standing Committee on Social Affairs, Science and Technology decided to look at how globalization and technology were affecting social cohesion.

I was one of the people called to be a witness for this committee. My trip to Ottawa started out in a typically Canadian fashion. The planes were all late because of a March snowstorm. I finally reached Ottawa, and after a nerve-wracking taxi ride through the snow storm, I reached the committee fifteen minutes late. They were all still there waiting to hear what I had to say. They listened, and were not pleased. Why was I so negative? Surely things could not be this bad. They had wanted to hear success stories, stories of hope, and of how people were being re-integrated into Canadian society. My message was that more and more of us were falling out, not being helped back in. And it was not possible to be re-integrated unless some radical changes were made by government.

My message was that global capitalism, and technological change, meant more and more workers with no work, or with a little work at destitution wages. The fact that we have no money means not only that we have no food, it means that we are pushed further and further out of any community. Whereas some Canadians have access to the whole world via the Internet, some Canadians cannot afford a phone. The battle for a telephone has been going on for as long as I have been aware of social policy issues. For at least thirty-five years people on welfare have been fighting to have money for a phone. If you have a medical problem, and need to contact a doctor, you can have money for a phone. Otherwise, you are out of luck. Your choice is food from the food bank, and then maybe enough money for a phone, or no phone.

The idea that many of us no longer have a phone, and that many of us would never again have access to a job at a living wage unless there were drastic changes, was incomprehensible to some of the senators. Liberal Senator Sister Peggy Butts questioned my plea for all Canadians to have access to the riches of this country. Her response was to tell me to get a job. I can laugh at this now, and it makes a good story when discussing the fate of the Senate. At the time I was dumbfounded. I continued with the discussion, and hoped that my words made sense while I regained my composure. On reflection, I wonder how we can build a society together when our leaders have such disdain for those who have been excluded. The answer is that those of us who care can build a society with different leaders, different values and a different belief system, or as some would say, a new paradigm.

As soon as we talk about new ways of looking at life and new ways of building a society, people's defences rise up. The great boogie man of "loss of our individual rights and freedoms" is usually waved around. Any talk of solidarity and the common good is met with the suspicion that something precious to us may be lost. Rather than ignoring the issue we need to struggle with it, and hopefully come to a deeper and more valuable way of understanding how people can live together. As Michael Ignatieff says, the most important question any society can ask is how to reconcile individual freedom and solidarity.

Many people are struggling to find a new and better way to answer that question. Anne Schaef, in her many books talks about alternative ways of living together, based on wisdom from aboriginal communities all over the world. In *Native Wisdom for White Minds* she says that it is through community support that we grow and thrive. Healthy individuals and societies are those in which each person knows that he or she has a particular place, and where mutual interdependence in community results in freedom.

Jean Vanier asks essentially the same question as Ignatieff.

"How can we have healthy individuals within a healthy group?" He maintains that the way to inner freedom and maturity is to break out of the hell of individualistic self-centeredness. His vision of what true freedom is, is a compelling one. Becoming oneself is never done at the expense of another person. For Vanier, personal freedom refuses to compromise with evil and the forces of oppression that crush others. He contrasts the idea of the individual's freedom to control and judge others, with the "freedom to take our own place and not anyone else's in society and the universe so as to live communion and compassion, and communicate trust and freedom to others." He calls this freedom of vulnerability, openness and listening to others the freedom to be ourselves, and this freedom happens in community.

Vanier not only writes about how to live in community, he practices living in community. His experiment into community began after a career in the Canadian army, in a monastic order in Spain, and after teaching philosophy at the Sorbonne in Paris. Vanier and a friend and two men who had been institutionalized because they were classified as "mentally retarded" began the first L'Arche community. Today there are L'Arche communities all over the world. These intentional communities have been set up as an alternative to institutions. These communities are based on the idea that we all have value, that we all have gifts and that we all are both beautiful and broken.

I have never lived in a L'Arche community, but I have occasionally been reminded of the truth of the L'Arche vision. One day I was riding the Portage bus on my way to downtown Winnipeg. The bus stopped at Polo Park shopping centre. A young man got on. He sat down at the front of the bus and began to talk to everyone around him. He had on a special jacket that announced that he was part of a CKY TV telethon.

He had just come from the TV station, and was so excited that he had been on TV. The young man had limited mental capacity, but an unlimited capacity to enjoy a new and exciting experience, and to share it with everyone around him. Soon all the people near him were asking him about his experience and enjoying his enthusiasm and excitement. When he got off the bus everyone had a smile on their face, and the day was brighter.

The groups within society, and the society as a whole, make decisions as to who will be included. Some major changes have occurred over the last fifty years. The boy on the bus is now accepted as a part of the larger society. He is in the community. If he is lucky he will also live in his own smaller community of a group home, possibly a L'Arche group home. Fortunately there are even projects designed to make sure that such individuals are not only "in" the community, but also part "of" the community. Inclusion means being connected with other people in the community. Project Friendship in Prince George, BC run by the Association for Community Living connects people with others in the community with similar interests and gifts. They are friends, not volunteers and clients.

It is possible to have healthy individuals within a healthy group. The question of my independent freedom is not seen as relevant if I do not fear my friends and neighbours. Rather, as Anne Schaef says, each person knows that they have a place. Community support enables each individual to grow and thrive. In community our very interdependence gives us freedom. Small groups of people here and there have accepted this vision of community. Community relationships, caring love for each other, are seen as something to strive for. This is a value for only a very small number of people, but I believe in the seed theory. Start small and grow. I look for and applaud every small example I find.

One example in Winnipeg is the Grain of Wheat community. People share a common religious understanding of community. They worship together, live in the Wolseley area of Winnipeg and share resources in a variety of ways. They have also opened the Tall Grass Prairie Bakery, a cooperative venture that uses only organic flour. There are other examples of people building communities in Canada. Jane Buchan writes of numerous examples in southern Ontario.[66] Susan Berlin writes about communities in BC.[67] In these examples, as in most examples of communities large and small, based on ideals or neighbourhoods, care of the environment is considered an essential component. Not only do we belong to each other, we belong in an eco-system. Jane Buchan says that sustainable practices are nothing less than expressions of love for our home, our human and non-human communities, and ourselves.

Community of the Non-Employed

I have spent a large part of my life striving for social justice and being part of a faith community. The two have seldom happened at the same time. However, from my experiences in the SCM in the 1960s I have always believed faith and justice belonged together. Creating the community does not mean that we become so inward looking that we no longer spend time and energy on the issues that brought us together. Rather, as Helen Forsey says "Communities can be a home base for carrying on the struggle."[68] I have always thought that a group needs to become a community in order to stay together and create change. This is harder than it sounds.

People have to have a number of things in common. A group of individuals becomes a community when they have a common belief system, common goals and values, common resources available, and when they participate together in common actions. How do you create a community with individuals who have no resources, little in common except the day to day struggle to survive, and whose main goal is to get a job and thus be re-integrated into the mainstream of society?

It took a crisis to begin CANE. At least it seemed like a crisis in the early 1990s. Jobs were disappearing. The cuts to Unemployment Insurance and welfare were just beginning. People were appalled and questioning this attack on the poor. The churches in Winnipeg began a Church and Community Inquiry into Unemployment. Many people from all sectors of society representing themselves or groups came and gave suggestions as to what we and the government should do. A number of us were at the Inquiry, and also met at a demonstration against UI cuts, and a demonstration at City Hall. We decided that more than demonstrations were necessary. We decided to form a group to continue the struggle. A common concern brought us together.

Most social justice groups begin with a common concern. There is a perception of a problem, and some idea of what needs to be done to change government policy. When we began CANE most of the people had never been involved in political action. They had no real analysis of what was happening. They knew that they and their families were being marginalized, but did not know why, or what to do about it. Before we decided to do anything, we decided to have a clear understanding of what we wanted to see happen. We spent six weeks working on a Mission Statement. This Mission Statement was based on the United Nations Declaration of Human Rights. Within our Mission Statement we identified three strategies, or focuses. They are support, education and advocacy. The community building is the support.

A Mission Statement outlining the goals of the group is

one way of creating a group identity. Every time we develop a new policy the group identity becomes stronger. One day one of our members was telling me about a discussion that occurred before I got to the Tuesday meeting. We had been planning a garage sale to raise money for trips to the country. One of the members suggested having a raffle at the sale. A number of other members said that CANE did not believe in any form of gambling. They discussed this for a while. The reasons for the policy were explained. The member who had suggested the raffle then agreed that they should not have a raffle because we did not support gambling for a good reason. We do not believe in competitive individualism, with one winner and the rest of us losers. Thus, CANE members do not support gambling.

Group identity is also shaped by how the group is run, and who has the power in the group. Who makes the decisions? At the very beginning of CANE there was a major split over this issue. Some of the members believed in a very authoritarian and hierarchical structure. Others believed in sharing power, and that everyone should have a voice. It became clear after a number of meetings that we had to choose which structure to use. The majority wanted to create a participatory democracy, although at the time we did not call it that. We decided to have a general meeting once a month, where all decisions by the Steering Committee are looked at. We only go ahead if the majority agree. We strive for consensus. After we all looked at Patrick Watson's television series called *The Struggle for Democracy* everyone agreed that we wanted a participatory democracy. This means that things take longer to accomplish. But it also means that everyone is heard and has a voice in decision making. People feel that their ideas are valued.

The result of this style of organization meant that those who wanted an authoritarian structure, with all decisions made by the leader and executive, left. This issue of power and structure was not decided once and for all at the beginning. It is so important that it is looked at and reaffirmed on a regular basis. We looked at the issues around power again when we were attempting to form a coalition with other groups in order to have a common response to the ongoing government cutbacks on programs and intensified controls on people. We wanted the coalition to include and value every member, whether paid staff or welfare recipient. We want everyone to feel their voice is important.

This is the key to community. Every person in the community is valued. Every person has a gift to offer the community, whether typing letters, or washing dishes, or looking after children, or preparing a brief to government. This concept is so foreign to our way of life. It is hard for people, especially those who are blamed and excluded, to believe that they have a gift to offer. We were discussing this idea one day at one of our Tuesday meetings. It was clear that many beliefs about the world, and who we are in the world, hindered our ability to participate fully in CANE. It was easy to identify the negative forces in our lives. It was very hard for most people to identify their gifts.

Community is also built on ritual and celebration. Native peoples come together in pow-wows. The traditional pow-wow is a spiritual gathering that strengthens community and that teaches reverence for and reciprocity for all creation. Anne Schaef says that community is the "playground where we move through the dance of life." At CANE we have the traditional celebrations of Christmas and Thanksgiving. We also mark special events. At our fifth Annual General Meeting we had a big supper, including a donated birthday cake from the Tall Grass Prairie Bakery.

Gandhi said that we should celebrate everything that

brings hope. Celebration means words of hope, laughter and singing and gifts. Every year we have a conference at CANE. We learn a lot, but more than that we celebrate. We laugh and sing and have good food. Harvey Cox has said that "Laughter is hope's last weapon." Laughter has come at the conferences, the retreats and at the Tuesday meetings of CANE. I remember the day that we realized that more than one of our members had thought about jumping off the top of the Richardson building on the corner of Portage and Main. The thought came from despair, but the group put up an imaginary diving board on the building and we ended in laughter. Here in Winnipeg we are blessed with laughter from the wit of Aboriginal peoples. *Joe from Winnipeg* is heard on CBC radio every Thursday morning. The native theatre troupe *As the Bannock Burns* shows ordinary native people struggling with white bureaucrats and native leaders. We laugh together at their vision of the absurdity of life.

Community is celebration, laughter, working together on common goals, but community is not achieved easily. Anyone who has tried to create a community knows that it can be a daunting task. People still make mistakes and hurt each other. At CANE there are arguments around everything from whether to have a conference this year to what should be served at Tuesday lunch. Within groups of people there is friction and disagreement. Within each person there is both the gift and the wounded spirit. Vanier speaks of us all as being both beautiful and broken. Henri Nowen writes of the wounded healer. How can people exist together creatively in a community when ongoing stress often results in anger and blaming?

It is only possible if there is love. The word "love," as Vanier and belle hooks and Martin Luther King use it encompasses the ideal of forgiveness and sacrifice. We know those qualities are essential in a family, but we forget that they are equally essential in any community of people. One day during a discussion two CANE members started to yell at each other. Later, during "check-in" one of the members apologized for her outburst, and the other said "That's okay, no offense taken." Forgiveness for harsh words means people can go on. The past is forgotten.

The Wider Community

I remember hearing a story about Mother Teresa. She was in New York in order to start one of her homes. Someone asked how she could do this when she had no money. Mother Teresa laughed and asked how you could imagine that there was no money in New York, one of the richest cities in the world. She assumed the money was there and would become available to her. It seems like we need a saint to access the riches in Canada, one of the richest countries in the world. The walls are so high between the haves and the have nots that little seems to get over them.

Another story I remember is found in Jean Vanier's book *Be Not Afraid*. He has a long poem that describes first the two worlds of misery and of riches, and then the wall between them:

> *Between these two worlds*
> *A huge wall*
> *which prevents direct contact*
> *meeting, communion*
> *sometimes there may be*
> *exchanges*
> *but never any direct contact*
> *The comfortable throw money*
> *or things over the wall*
> *but the last thing*

they want
is to see or touch
They send roses
they don't give them
they throw them
over the wall
faded roses
almost dead
but they look like a present

Sometimes the resources we are given are stale bread and dead roses. But sometimes the bread is fresh and the roses smell so sweet. Occasionally, real gifts are given. One day a woman from the Royal Winnipeg Ballet phoned up and asked if we would like some tickets. A group of us went to the Nutcracker at Christmas. At our Annual Conference last year one of the union people I know walked in at lunch time with a cheque for $250 dollars from his local. My church community has given us $500 dollars for our retreat *Discovering our Gifts*. They have donated lots of treasures for the CANE garage sale. Money from the sale was used for day trips to the country. Such gifts from friends and strangers in the wider community are appreciated and valued. They are resources that enable our community to celebrate that life is good.

It is the resources for the struggle for justice that are lacking. One of the barriers to people and foundations giving us money is that we lack a charity number. According to the rules we can not get a charity number, because we are an advocacy group. So I continue to harass and beg from all my friends and acquaintances. The money to pay the monthly phone bill and bus tickets to our vigil or to our office has to be raised month after month.

Occasionally the wider community reaches out to the marginalised in order to draw them into the circle. In 1997 I got a call from John Friesen, one of my union friends. He told me that his union, the Canadian Union of Postal Workers (CUPW), was opening up the Workers Organizing Resource Centre. This is a centre whose goal is to organize the unorganized, and to fight for justice for all workers. He offered CANE office space, and all the things that go with it, like a photocopier, fax, and office supplies. CUPW has not only provided office space, it has provided a focal point for people to gather and talk and plan activities around a wide variety of justice issues. There is a cross section of community activities in the office. The other people and groups are focused on planning activities, rather than forming a community . This seems to be the focus it will continue to have because the analyses and strategies of the different groups are so various. But we all care about justice and are struggling to understand each other and to work together. The exciting aspect about WORC is that both marginalized workers and those with union jobs are working together. The people who suffer injustice are respected and included.

The issue of solidarity with the oppressed is also recognized by a large group in the United States. People there are now beginning to feel the repercussions of the welfare bill made law a few years ago. More and more people are being thrown off welfare. There is a report from the Third Annual Pentecost to Overcome Poverty.[69] The speakers are reported to urge all people, including those living in poverty, to be involved in radical social action. It is reported in the last session that if one message could be synthesized from the conference, it would be the repeated admonition to include poor people in the movement to overcome poverty.

The principle of actually living in communities with people living in poverty was also discussed. This is an old and honourable tradition. A famous example was Dorothy Day and the Catholic Worker Movement. Today in Winnipeg four Grey Nuns moved onto Langside Street in the West Broadway area, one of our most notorious streets. One of the sisters is an active member of CANE. This small example of people choosing to be with people in poverty is a gift to me, and to the other members of CANE. When things get discouraging I can walk over to the house for a cup of tea, conversation, prayer on the third floor chapel, by myself, or with the others in the house. Shared concern in a place of love still exists. It is precious because it is so rare.

My Community

We all want to belong to something bigger than ourselves. We want relationships with others. We yearn for community. We are constantly faced with the alternative vision of competitive individualism. Thus, we have to consciously decide to make community a priority in our lives. You know that community has reached the top of your priority list when you start to give your time to it. We always have the time for the things that we believe are most important. Robert and I gave building our family community our top priority when our children were young. At this point in my life seeking justice for all means working to build a society where everyone is included, where everyone is part of the human family. The human community also includes the earth in which we live.

At the point of discovering a shared vision we encounter excitement, commitment and spirit.

For any community to grow it must contain both a vision that is shared and that is big enough to allow for creative diversity. This creative diversity becomes visible when people put together short-term tasks. A focused team of people from within the larger group can implement a project that is valued and supported by the larger group. For example, CANE can put on a CANE Conference, or St. Margaret's Anglican church can put on a Fall Festival for the people in the neighbourhood. The two essential components for any community are diversity within the group and an outward focus for the group

The final step in forming community is the transition from "the community for myself" to "myself for the community." This is only possible when we have chosen love, when we are willing to sacrifice, and when we are willing to forgive. This is real freedom, internal freedom, and this is found in community. Vanier calls it a passing from a land of slavery to the promised land.

CHAPTER 11
HOPE
SPRINGS ETERNAL

We need critical hope the way a fish needs unpolluted water.
PAULO FREIRE, *Pedagogy of Hope*

What I am arguing against is the politics based on easy hopes about the future human situation.
GEORGE GRANT, *Critique of the New Left*

I BEGAN MY SEARCH FOR HOPE by remembering despair. I went back and read over Chapter Three: Don't Get Your Hopes Up. As I did that, my reaction was to relive all the pain. I remembered the weeks and months and years of looking at and recording all my pain, and the pain of my friends in CANE. I wondered if I would ever be able to find a way past the pain. How does anyone get past the pain and sorrow of loss? Finally, it became clear to me that the first section of my book was actually a process of mourning. Mourning includes fear, anger, guilt and despair. Everything seems disorganized, and we seek to make sense of our losses. We struggle to understand what is happening. Thankfully, others have been on this journey before us, and have shared their experiences, and what they have learned.

Bill McKibben[70] had been writing about the crisis in the environment, and had discovered that his writings had led people to fear and discouragement He had spent years researching and writing about the destruction of our planet. His book,

The End of Nature, depressed him and his readers so much that he realized that fear and despair changes nothing. He realized that what people needed was hope. What he and others had been doing for so long was grieving for the planet. Now he was ready to say "I'm done mourning." We all have to truly mourn, to grieve what has happened to us, our friends and neighbours, before we can begin to hope. Now it is time to move on. Now I too can say that "I'm done mourning."

Unfortunately, some people stay in that place of mourning. The result can be fatigue, hyperactivity, inability to focus or to concentrate. Some people turn to addictions and sadly some feel so overwhelmed they choose suicide. Occasionally we are reminded of how deep the pain can be. At one of our Tuesday meetings Sister Rolande came to tell us that one of the people from the area had committed suicide. She had not been a member of CANE, but many of us knew her. She would come to the Drop-In when we were having our Tuesday meetings. She never joined us, but wandered around the group circle, always on the outside, even though she was invited in. The response to her death was a sudden and dramatic disclosure by other CANE members that they too had considered suicide. We immediately began to consider ways to be available for each other when someone desperately needed some support. We are not crisis counselors, but we can be friends who listen. One of our members was delegated to check on kinds of answering machines that could be accessed from another phone. We decided to set up a system so that a phone call would be returned within twenty-four hours.

For some the decision is not to physically kill oneself, but to spiritually die, to turn away from hope. They have been disappointed too often. They decide that it is better not to hope. At least if you do not hope you will not be disappointed once again. This choice is called fatalism. The educator Paulo Freire talks about fatalism and the people who choose it. He gives examples both from the Third World and inner cities in the United States. The belief is that nothing can or will change. He gives the example of one man who talked about living in a nightmare from which he will never awaken. Many people remain in the nightmare. The form the nightmare takes is varied. It can be social isolation, addiction or just sleepwalking through life.

One of the reasons why people who are marginalized remain stuck in the grief nightmare is because this grief is never taken seriously. It is never even acknowledged. I checked the library shelves. There are tons of books on grief. They deal with our own, or a loved one's, death or dying, or with physical or mental suffering. Except for a few paragraphs here and there no one seems to have taken seriously the tremendous sense of loss experienced by those who have lost their job, their income, their place in society.

I started to ask people in CANE whether they had grieved for their losses. There was immediate and dramatic responses. I stopped asking in order to consider how this pain could be dealt with in a helpful, supportive way. I realized that we had never taken this issue seriously, maybe because no one else does. For those who have lost everything, the pain of mourning is discounted. We are told to have exactly the opposite emotional response. Everyone is ordered to put on a happy face and get out there and search for work. Everyone is told that their hope lies in finding a job at a living wage.

False Hope: The Hope of Results

A member of CANE came into the office. He was incensed, enraged at the system. He had been to yet another program for the unemployed. He had hoped that their assessment and the seven week course they offered would lead to a job, but after the assessment he was not even allowed to take the course. There were too many others ahead of him with better qualifications. He kept saying that they had promised to help and there was no help. He kept saying "They give false hope. They give false hope."

Dare I say that the hope of results is a false hope. What heresy it is to consider that the hope of results will let us down. We live in a world that believes in identifying a goal, picking your means to reach the goal, working hard and inevitably the goal will be achieved and the hoped for result will happen. For the young adult seeking his first job, for the older laid off worker, for the under-employed or non-employed the same goal beckons. All have the goal of a well-paid secure job. I have heard people express the hope of reaching this goal countless times. Everything in our society tells us it is possible if we follow the right formula. We believe in "technique." There is the right means to achieve our ends. So people get an appropriate education, go to the job-finding club, get their resume done again and again.

If the goal is not reached people are told they have not followed the formula correctly, and to start again. It is not even considered possible that the goal is unreachable. I have been told by staff in labour adjustment programs that they will not tell laid off workers about CANE. The reason they give is that the laid off workers have to keep hoping for a new union job. The very existence of CANE means that this hope will not be realized for some of the people they are helping.

We know that some goals are reachable. The very fact that some people do reach their goals is enough to prove that it can be done, and people who have caught the golden ring want to encourage others that it can be done. The people who achieve their goals, often despite horrendous obstacles, want to share their successes. They want to help others also achieve their goals. The first time I encountered this well meaning reaching out to others was at the Workers Centre in Kitchener. I was in town for a conference on Empowerment, and decided to walk over to the Centre. There was a group of non-employed workers meeting there. There was also a former member of the group who had gotten a job. He came back to the group in order to give the others hope. If he could get a job, then they also could get a job. The focus was on getting a job and the sign of hope for this group was that one of the members had actually achieved this goal.

We can find many examples of success for individuals, or for groups that have been marginalized. I happened to see on the TV the first graduating class from the Native American Prep school in the United States. These young Native Americans were given the opportunity to be a part of a rigorous high school education that encompassed their culture. They were going on to universities such as Yale. The young people were planning and dreaming to help their people when they finished their education. For them and their families this school was a sign of hope.

Where we get trapped is confusing the sign with the hope. Just as it is folly to base one's faith on miracles, it is folly to base one's hope on the signs of success. We can rejoice in goals reached after much struggle, but we have to acknowledge that goals may be reached tomorrow, or years from now. They may be reached by us, or by our children or friends. The dreams and the struggles are always there. The concrete results may or may not happen for us. There is nothing wrong with having goals. There are goals worth striving for, but if our hope resided in achieving the goals, in the results of the striving, then failure, for whatever reason, leads to despair.

The formula, the technique, of setting and reaching goals is followed by individuals seeking a well paying secure job, but also by individuals seeking a just society and jobs for all. Social activists are seduced by the hope of results just as much as the job seeker. When we reflect on the failures of this technique we would do well to consider the words of Thomas Merton.[71] He said "Do not depend on the hope of results. When you are doing the sort of work you have taken on . . . you may have to face the fact that your work will be apparently worthless and even achieve no result at all, if not perhaps results opposite to what you expect. As you get used to this idea, you start more and more to concentrate not on the results, but on the value, the rightness, the truth of the work itself."

The Power of Hope

Why should we seek signs whenever we talk of hope? For the paradox of hope is that it is present when all looks hopeless. When evil people and systems, powers visible and invisible, appear to be in control that is precisely when hope is desperately needed. Thus hope must be full of power to be of any use at all. Our tragedy is that we have forgotten the power of hope. The word has been used too often to mean a wish. McKibben says the word has been debased into usage in sentences such as, "I hope the scientists are wrong about global warming." "I hope everything will turn out okay." If hope is such a weak and wishy-washy thing, it is useless to us. If hope has no power, then why not turn to fatalism, or cynicism, or sleeping by night and sleep-walking by day?

Thankfully, once we recognize and discard the weak and false hopes we are free to embrace the true hope, the hope of power. This is the hope that Freire says originates in the very nature of human beings. This is the hope that is so powerful that it is present in the most hopeless of situations. Through the writings of people such as Victor Frankel, Corrie Ten Boom, and others we know that hope was present in the Nazi concentration camp. We read that those who had hope lived, and those who did not died. In the 1960s there was an abundance of thinking and writing about hope. Hope was in the air. Jessie Jackson, one of the leaders of the civil rights movement in the United States led his people with the slogan "Keep Hope Alive." There were writers such as Paulo Freire and Thomas Merton, and in Canada George Grant explored what hope meant. Hope was present in Nelson Mandela's prison cell. Hope has always been present in leaders of vast movements such as Gandhi and Martin Luther King. Hope was, and is, always possible in the lives of the ordinary person struggling to make sense of disaster, pain and suffering.

How is it possible? The secret of hope's power and presence is that hope does not stand alone. It is intrinsically bound together with faith and love. All those who have written of hope from the places of hell have made this clear. They have linked hope to faith and love, forgiveness and sacrifice. They understood that each life is precious and has meaning. Victor Frankel in the Nazi prison camp told his comrades not to lose hope, but to have courage. The focus of his message was that life under any circumstance never ceases to have meaning. The very sacrifice of their lives, their suffering and their death had meaning. He believed that love is ultimately the highest goal. Corrie Ten Boom also spoke of, and lived, love and forgiveness from Auschwitz.

Gandhi spoke of, and lived, love and forgiveness. His guiding force was "satyagraha." This concept means that when bad times come, you shed tears and you mourn. It also means that we celebrate everything that brings hope, and that we forgive the injustice and those who have been responsible for it. Freire also speaks of faith and hope together. He considers this way of living as necessary in order to counteract the forces of fatalism. For fatalism helps the dominant, and hope is part of "the spurring faith of loving rebelliousness."

CRITICAL HOPE

Freire has been writing about oppression and hope for thirty years. He was still writing about it in 1997, long after most people had given up talking about hope. He takes seriously all the pain and loss and suffering of people. And yet he says "I reject the notion that nothing can be done about the consequences of economic globalization, and refuse to bow my head gently because nothing can be done against the unavoidable." We can see the best and the worst, and still move forward creatively, with hope. This hope is called "critical hope."

Critical hope means careful judgement. It broadens and deepens the concept of hope and encompasses all the power of hope. It encompasses a whole way of living. Critical hope begins with understanding, by which Freire means understanding the words and the facts we gather within their context. This is how we discover the truth. Second, there is the vision for "without a vision, hope is impossible." Then there is the work and the waiting. Finally we have the outcome, the result. The result is never pre-determined, as those who believe in mechanical, technical control would have us believe. The outcome is mystery, surprise and gift.

a) Discovering the Truth

When CANE began we decided that a resource library would be

---

a very important tool to have. A number of us worked diligently setting up a library. We clipped articles from the newspapers, photocopied articles from magazines, added some of our own books to the CANE library. Others thought that a place where information on poverty and unemployment was available would be valuable. Soon after we started there was a large gathering of anti-poverty activists at the West Broadway Community Centre. We were exploring strategies and debating how to move forward. One of the suggestions was to have a resource library. Most of the people there thought this would be a great idea. So I said that CANE had already started one, and that we would be happy to share it with the community. We have continued to expand this library. It is now located in the Workers Organizing Resource Centre, where it is available to everyone who comes into the centre. We continue to receive articles and magazines. Whenever a new resource came in I pointed it out to our members. To be honest, the whole experiment seems to have been a waste of time. Only a few people in the group and in the larger community ever look at anything in the library.

I prepared a library full of really interesting information about the society we live in, and what is happening in that society. It seems that this information is of little interest to most of the people who are marginalized. Is the lack of interest in learning about our society and how it works a symptom of the fatalism of those who struggle to survive? Or is the lack of interest the norm? I think that the people in CANE are not really much different from the average Canadian. Outside of educational institutions, various "think tanks" of the Left and Right, and a small handful of social activists, most make do with TV sound bites to make sense of the world. The powers that be, those in positions of power, of domination, have used that power to convince most oppressed people that there is nothing to be done. The future will be more of the same. The politicians are all the same. The media accepts what is. The people have accepted fatalism as the only reasonable philosophy. We do not call it fatalism. We call it accepting reality.

Given that social analysis is not high on anyone's priority list, I have found that people do want to learn. They just do not always want to learn what I think they should learn. It seems so obvious upon reflection that we start where people are, but we have been trained into the authoritarian model of education that assumes those in power know what other people need and want to know. I was reminded of the standard education model last month when I took a computer course. It was for women involved in non-profit organizations. I knew most of what they taught us, but did learn a few new things. The course was for three hours for eight afternoons, or for twenty-four hours. I could have learned what I wanted to know in two hours, but it was standard education. Everyone progressed along learning the same things at the same rate. There was no concern with what I wanted or needed to know, or with what I already knew when I entered the course. The whole experience got me started thinking about education.

Modern education, whether the school system, or computer training courses, or job-finding clubs, is based on the premise that everyone starts at the same place and is marched through the curriculum at the same pace. We are expected to arrive at the end of the process with our heads full of the same facts. In this Information Age we certainly have enough facts to find. And the facts are expanding at an overwhelming rate. The problem is that they are unrelated facts with no context. Obvious examples are statistical facts that taken by themselves mean nothing. The fact that the unemployment rate is a certain number tells us nothing unless we know how many discouraged workers there are, what percentage of workers are in the labour market, how many jobs are part-time, etc. When George Grant was warning about "easy hopes" he was warning us that we have opted for fact finding and technological mastery to discover the truth.

Those who encourage us to discover the truth about the society we live in are quite clear that this truth seeking is hard work. It requires deep and careful thought. Michael Czerny and Jamie Swift[72] say that the purpose of critical thinking is to find the truth. They define critical thinking as developing a discerning attitude, a habit of trying to get to the bottom of things. They talk about asking critical questions that lead to an awareness of previously unsuspected connections.

George Grant has acknowledged how hard it is to discover the truth of things precisely because we are snowed under by the avalanche of unconnected facts. But he adds one more element that is essential to finding the truth. He says that we are likely the first recorded civilization with the arrogance to believe that we can dismiss theology and philosophy as having nothing to say about truth.

b) Dreaming the Dream

Once the grieving for the past is finished, and the analysis of the present is complete, it is time to dream the future into being. For the fatalist who believes the future is just the continuation of the past, this is an impossibility. For those of us who live in hope, a totally new and different future is waiting to be born. Hope means looking at the future, seeing our lives and our communities and our world as we want them to be and believing that it is possible. There are many parts to critical hope, but the dream, the vision, is the part that makes our hearts sing and our hopes soar. The dream carries us forward when all logic and reason and "reality" tell us it is hopeless. The dream carried Martin Luther King to the mountaintop.

Martin Luther King had a dream of freedom for his people. The dream is always of freedom, but the meaning of freedom changes. Obviously, people and groups have very different ideas of what freedom means. Our ideas about freedom come from our value base and our world view. Although most of us are not aware that we have a world view, it is, as Walter Wink says, the foundation for our myths, symbols and systems of thought.

The dominant world view today is comprised of two interrelated ideologies - individualism and materialism. Both individualism and materialism are connected through the atomic theory, that is, that everything is made up of atoms, individual bits of matter. Rick Salutin says that we live in a world of disconnected facts, and that everything is a matter of personal choice.[73] Thus, for people who hold the dominant world view and who embrace individualism, freedom means the freedom to have as many consumer goods and services as possible, and the freedom to do whatever you want within legal limits. Belle hooks recognizes how hard it is to make the shift away from materialism. She says that what makes it so hard is that many equate freedom with materialism.

Both capitalism and communism come from the world view of materialism. The capitalists try to dismantle government so that there are fewer and fewer legal limits. They see government as having power that is destructive and enslaving. On the other hand the communist sees the multinational corporations as the destructive power that enslaves us. The ideology of materialism began to dominate our thinking at the time of the Enlightenment in the 18th Century. The materialist world view says that we can only know reality through our five senses. There is no spirit. The battle between communism and capitalism wages within a common view that dismisses spirit. Our challenge is to find and articulate a new world view, a new paradigm. When we we are able to we will have a new definition of what freedom means.

Thirty years ago Walter Wink began his struggle to understand and come to terms with destructive enslaving power. He visited many countries. He went to South Africa, and South and Central America in the 1980s. He talked to the tortured, and the families of those who had disappeared. He talked to the priests and nuns who daily struggled for human rights and political freedom. The result was that he was overwhelmed by anger and despair and became physically sick. In his despair he turned to the New Testament. He read that "neither death, nor life, nor angels, nor principalities, nor powers will be able to separate us from the love of God in Christ Jesus." He found a "thin thread of hope," and clung to it. He has spent the time since then naming and struggling with the Powers. In this struggle he came to articulate a new world view that he calls an Integral World View. Matter and spirit are two parts of the same reality. Reality has an inner and outer aspect. Thus the Powers That Be are both visible and invisible, both office towers and corporate culture. All the Powers are linked together in a complex network that he calls the Domination System.

I feel like I am in a time loop. After thirty years I am back challenging The System. In the 1960s there was much talk about challenging The System, but that analysis gradually disappeared. In a few places people continued to talk about The System. In South Africa when the police came to the door, people inside would warn "The System is here." But here in Canada I have not heard talk of The System for thirty years. In the 1960s we talked about wanting to be free from The System.

There were some key components to The System that were challenged. University students in Canada marched against nuclear weapons. Some joined the fight against the Vietnam war and against racism. Some focused on transforming the universities. Often this meant a fight for universities to hire Canadian professors. In the end the only changes to The System were things such as token students on university boards. The System itself chugs on as usual.

The problem was that we had so little idea of what exactly the old system was and what exactly a new system might look like. Walter Wink and others have now identified the old system. He and belle hooks have identified it as the system of domination. Walter Wink's dream is focused on freedom from the Domination System, the internal and external manifestations of the Powers that Be. He also dreams of freedom for the Powers, that they be transformed. Anne Schaef's dream is to free people to be able to Live in Process.

Wink, hooks, and Schaef are not the only dreamers. I have found the dreams of freedom in the prayers of the peoples of the world. In the book *Prayers for a Thousand Years* we find "a collection of empowering visions for a common future and a celebration of the infinite varieties of human hope." In the book over two hundred and fifty teachers, activists, leaders and visionaries share their dreams for the future. The dreams and visions of the new world come from the spiritual teachers and leaders of all the world's faith communities. Christians such as Matthew Fox and Buddhists such as Joanna Macy have here and elsewhere written creatively about new dreams. Anne Schaef and many others draw on Aboriginal teachings to lead us to a new and better way of seeing the world. I was looking at a library book of pictures by Native artist Frank Howell. Beside the picture of Raven was a poem by Michael French.

"Despite angry winters, wild flowers grow. Despite the never-ending night, there is still a light. The grandfather's light — a hand to a path for tomorrow."

We engage in the struggle for clarity for a new vision, a new paradigm, a new dream of freedom. There is to be no common articulated vision that we can identify. Rather, there seems to be the strands of a vast tapestry slowly being woven together into a pattern. I live in hope that the dreamers will complete the pattern. Then there will be a new dream of freedom for us all.

c) Working and Waiting

There is more than the dreaming. Paulo Freire says that the future of which we dream is not inexorable. We have to make it, produce it, else it will not come in the form that we would wish it to. Neither the dreaming, nor the work will move forward as long as we are caught in despair. Bill McKibben recognized this trap after he wrote *The End of Nature*. He found that he and everyone else who read it got really depressed. He realized that fear and despair were not going to result in people working for change. The problems seem so overwhelming that most people just close down, block out, run away. McKibben recognized that what we needed was hope. What we need "is a vision of recovery, of renewal, of resurgence." So he wrote *Hope, Human and Wild*. He recognized that stories of success would give us hope.

People have not only written about new dreams and visions, they have struggled to put the spiritual and the material reality together. There has been a few places where this struggle has been recognized and valued. The Right Livelihood Foundation gives out the Right Livelihood Awards, which have been called the Alternative Nobel Prize. It is given to individuals and movements seeking to develop new visions of society, and to experiment in practical ways with new lifestyles, new paths of development and new relations with nature. All who receive this award "believe in diversity, and challenge the world view of a monochrome future of endless consumerism."

When we see examples of places, communities and nature where positive change has happened we see that maybe we can bring about change in our communities. We look for what work we can do. There is no doubt that there is work, "hard unending work." In fact, McKibben admits there is enough work to last a lifetime. Funnily enough, this is an exciting idea for me. For what else would we do with our lifetime?

The work may be physical action, demonstrating, lobbying, organizing. Or the work may be waiting. Jacques Ellul says that the person of hope is the person who waits. This is not an empty, passive, drowsy waiting, but a demanding wide-awake waiting. McKibben also talks about the need for waiting. He says that he does not mean a passive waiting, doing nothing. Rather our waiting for the right time to act involves "quiet moments for laying plans, for collecting ideas and solutions that will form the basis of the next environmental debate." He says that "for those concerned about the environment this is a strange season of waiting, a hard time for hope." Like a comet orbiting the earth, widespread concern for the environment comes into view only periodically.

For those of us waiting for the people of Canada to once again care for their neighbours as themselves, we will continue to prepare, to be ready for when there is once again a debate. We can learn about this waiting time from others. There was a story in *The Long Haul*, the newspaper put out by End Legislated

Poverty from BC. The story was written in an effort to encourage those fighting for a better world. Sandy Cameron, the author recognized that people get depressed because often it seems that nothing is happening. Her example was of a group of black women in Montgomery, Alabama. They were fighting for better conditions for black people on city buses. Cameron writes that in 1954 these women had prepared to distribute 50,000 notices calling people to boycott the buses. Only the time and place had to be added. In December, 1955 Rosa Parks refused to stand up in a Montgomery bus when ordered to give her seat to a white person. When the Women's Political Council heard that Rosa Parks had been arrested they were ready with their leaflets. The Civil Rights movement took off. Cameron concludes her article with an encouragement to keep going and "when the tide changes, we will be ready."

Being ready is a hard concept for us. We want to get it done now. Many years ago I remember being at a retreat at Gimli, Manitoba conducted by Jean Vanier. He made fun of how fast we had to do everything, even eat. This sense of getting everything done faster and faster is connected to our sense of time as linear. In order to get anything done we have to move as fast as possible from A to B. Waiting is only possible when we have a sense of time as Kairos, the right time. McKibben says that the gulf between cyclical and linear time is more profound than the gulf between communism and capitalism.

One of my favourite examples of waiting for the right time is a little experiment in pushing the government to consider allowing people to grow hemp. In 1996 CANE hired four students through the government's Green Team program. They had to have a project connected to the environment. So they decided to write a brochure about jobs and the environment geared towards high school students. As the project evolved I realized that the team was suggesting that the way of the future was to grow hemp. There are countless ways to use hemp, and it is an environmentally friendly crop. I knew that they were ahead of their time, and that the government bureaucrats, who were overseeing the project, would never agree to this suggestion. I was right. All references to hemp were to be eliminated from the brochure, or it would not be printed. I was reminded of the project this month when I saw a book called *Hemp Horizons – The Comeback of the World's Most Promising Plant*. It outlined how hemp can be grown without pesticides, how it can replace wood, cotton and petrochemical based fibers. The Green Team's work on information about hemp was important and valuable, and may have contributed to some Manitoba government official looking at this issue seriously. The waiting for that to happen is hard. The students were right, but the time was not right.

When we believe in our dream we can wait, as well as work. Robert saw the Dalai Lama on PBS TV the other day. He talked about non-violence as the way to achieve freedom for his people. He said that he believes in non-violence and teaches it. At the same time he recognizes that it does not seem to affect the Chinese who occupy his homeland of Tibet. Nevertheless, he continues to believe in it and preach it. The Dalai Lama's dream is for more than his homeland. He writes a message in Joanna Macy's book *Coming Back to Life – Practices to Reconnect Our Lives, Our World*. He says that it is no longer appropriate to think only of my village, my country or nation. The problems we face call for a "sense of universal responsibility rooted in love and kindness for our human brothers and sisters." He challenges us to think more clearly and to act. He embodies critical hope – thinking clearly, dreaming the dream, acting and waiting.

Signs of Solid Ground

Forgive me friends
if I appear hopeful,
Sure of myself. . .
I am moved by the joy
of discovering
right in the middle of the flood,
a flood which goes on and on
and which grows worse —
Signs of solid ground,
A place to plant
my olive branch.

A little pamphlet called *Learning from the Poor* says that to confront the evils of oppression is a spiritual activity. It concludes with this poem by Archbishop Helder Camero of Brazil called *The Song of Hope*. The poem is on a poster showing a dove with an olive branch in its beak as it flies over the flooded earth.

Originally I ended this chapter with Archbishop Camero's poem. I had looked for hope and finally I believed that hope was possible. People who had suffered immeasurably over the ages, all over the world have witnessed to that hope. My belief in hope was an intellectual belief and a faith that hope was possible, but I did not feel hopeful. I did not have Archbishop Camero's joy of seeing signs of solid ground.

Hope is linked to faith and love. Hope is also linked to peaceful strength. As long as I held on to my anger I would not be able to fully experience and to feel hope. The final stage on my journey has been to understand and transform my anger into peaceful strength. Once I explored and experienced the transformation that I recount in Chapter Twelve, I could return to my search for hope without it being tainted. As I finally realize who I am, I am able to experience the feeling of hope.

In the 1960s we sang a song. "Last night I had the strangest dream. I never dreamt before. I dreamed that men had all agreed to put an end to war." Last night I woke up in the middle of the night. I felt a connection to all the sources of hope, to all the dreamers, to an unseen power that is present underneath and beyond the darkness. I know now the feeling of hope.

CHAPTER 12

PEACEFUL STRENGTH:
The Power of the People

To understand power and the sources of violence we must ask ourselves what it means to be a human being.

ROLLO MAY,
Power and Innocence- A Search for the Sources of Violence

We are not paragons of peaceableness, but wounded, violent, frightened people trying to become human. We are not wan saints incapable of evil, but plain people clad in both light and dark, under the banner of love, seeking to be spiritual warriors.

Walter Wink,
The Powers That Be: Theology for a New Millennium

FOR MONTHS WE AT CANE had been waiting for the axe to finally fall and it finally did. The Manitoba Conservative government brought in Workfare legislation. An election was on the horizon, and the government was busily introducing a variety of "get tough" legislation. My first response was to feel sick to my stomach. My second response was anger. Before I had time to recognize, and then change my anger into a more positive and creative state, the media were phoning. CBC TV called up and asked me to come down and to take part in a panel discussion. I jumped at the chance. I wanted an opportunity to express my violent opposition to this oppressive legislation.

I walked into the CBC building on Portage Avenue. I was directed to the make-up room. Nothing fancy happens there. My hair was combed and a bit of lipstick applied. Next on to the waiting room. I did not know who else was going to be on the panel, and I was a little nervous. But in walked Sid Frankel, a professor at the School of Social Work. We had worked on many committees concerning poverty issues over the years. I knew he was articulate and knowledgeable on the issue, and that he was a good choice. Then in walked Rev. Harry Lahotsky, a Conservative candidate in the upcoming provincial election. I had to force myself to be civil to the man. He represented the government that had brought in the new mean spirited and punitive laws. Before we got into a heated discussion Ross Rutherford breezed in. We had all seen him before as he was one of the hosts of *24 Hours*, the local CBC nightly news show. He is a big man, much bigger in person than he appears on television. He had a smile on his face, was completely at ease and told us we could call him Rosco.

Now we got down to business. We were shown into the taping room, miked up and sound checks were done. We did not know what the questions would be, or what the focus of the interview would be. The trick in all media interviews is to get your points across regardless of the questions asked. This is a skill that I am still learning. As the discussion progressed it was clear that the struggle between the three of us was the struggle for authority, and each of us was arguing from our particular perspective. We each spoke from a different authority base. Sid was an expert on studies and statistics. He could articulate how and why workfare did not work. It had not worked in the United States, and it had not worked in the Canadian provinces where it was used. The goal was to reduce unemployment. The reality was that one group of unemployed was replaced by another group.

Unionized workers were replaced by former welfare recipients. The studies and statistics had no effect on Lahotsky. He argued that he knew "these people." He worked with them every day. He held their heads when they vomited from various drug overdoses. He knew that they had to be controlled and if they did not "straighten up," they had to be punished. He argued this from his particular brand of Christianity. We were told that we had no right to challenge this analysis. He was the authority on this subject.

Every word he uttered was an affront to me. The people on welfare that I knew were decent, struggling, and working hard just to survive. They are my friends. Their biggest hope is work at a living wage. How dare he stereotype people on welfare as addicts who needed to be controlled. And how dare he justify it from a Christian perspective. I challenged his analysis and his authority. I consider my understanding of the Christian faith to be just as valid as his. My faith is deeply personal, and based on years of study. I have spent a lifetime studying the causes of poverty and possible solutions. My understanding of human behaviour is based on system theory, not behaviourism. I believe people are motivated from the inside, not from carrots and sticks. When I tried to explain my perspective, and my basis of authority I was discounted. There is no doubt that being discounted and being talked down to is a recipe for outrage. When my family and I later watched the interview, it had been edited. My comments were adequate, and to the point. Later Robert said to me "You sure were angry." I was.

The next morning, I turned on the TV and watched Valerie Pringle interviewing a panhandler named Sean. He was part of a court challenge initiative to strike down the laws prohibiting people from panhandling. He was wise and funny, articulate and informed. There was no bitterness. There was some sadness when he talked about the talk radio, or rather " the hate radio show" that he had been on the previous day. Most of all I recognized that he was not angry. He did not hate the people in our society who were persecuting those at the bottom who were suffering..

When I compared the two interviews it was a shock. There was no question that Sean's quiet, thoughtful, but passionate concern was far more effective than my interview filled with righteous indignation It was clear to me that even though I had explored where my anger came from, and I had realized how destructive anger was, nothing had changed. I continued to react in powerless rage. Every time the government, with the support or indifference of large parts of the population, made the lives of those living in poverty just a little harder, my body began to react. My heart raced, and my body tensed. The fight mechanism kicked in. That extreme reaction became easy to identify. My anger was painfully obvious.

There must be a reason why I was still stuck in anger. Although my rational mind had decided that I did not want to continue being angry, at some level I must still have thought that anger was a good thing. Why would I, and most other people, consider anger a good thing? Anger is considered good because it gives us a shot of energy, and energy equates with power. Is it possible that some forms of energy are actually bad for us?

I can think of one obvious example of high energy that is not healthy. Everyone knows about the sugar high, especially mothers who have to cope with children who have had too many treats. I started thinking about people eating a candy bar in order to get some energy. I started talking to Robert about sugar and eating sensibly. We are both concerned about too much sugar in our diets because both our fathers developed diabetes in their fifties. After we eat sugar, or carbohydrates, it goes into the blood stream as blood sugar. This gives us energy. But too much blood sugar is poisonous, so the body produces insulin in order to bring the blood sugar level down. As the blood sugar level gets lower we experience a lack of energy. This, of course, leads us to eat more sugar in order to get more energy. Sugar does give us energy but it is transient, and it is followed by a low. There is a roller coaster effect of high, then low energy. Eventually our bodies break down with diabetes or other physical problems.

Anger is the emotionally equivalent to sugar. Anger also gives us a high. If we look at the world as a place filled with bad people doing bad things the anger is constantly fed into our system. This, of course, is easy to do. All we have to do is live on a steady diet of the nightly news. Many people no longer pay attention to the news because they know that sooner or later the emotional roller coaster that we are on will take us down to despair. If we spend enough time on this roller coaster finally we will break down emotionally. This is often called burn out.

I was now determined to transform my anger into something else, something powerful but positive. I began to search for the keys to this transformation. The search was two fold. I would go back to the library and research how others dealt with anger, and I would talk to the people around me.

The Search

I started at the place I had come to in my initial look at anger. Anger is the response of a powerless victim. I wondered how common this state of powerlessness was. How pervasive was it? Who is writing about this? So I went to my favourite resource person, Robert. He suggested I read Michael Lerner. Back to the library I went, and sure enough there was Lerner's book

Surplus Powerlessness. To my delight he has an overview of the issue that encompasses the US experience from the 1960s to today

Michael Lerner, in *Surplus Powerlessness* begins by outlining the class dominated culture of the United States. Lerner's work reintroduces the concept of the ruling class. There are a group of people who have real power. There are also vast public and private bureaucratic institutions that continue to grow bigger and bigger with globalization, and that have more and more power. Add to that the overwhelming media presence and power. Even in democracies there are people and institutions that have an awful lot of power and control over our lives.

Surplus powerlessness does not refer to any of these external controls over people. Rather it refers to the fact that we are made powerless by our own beliefs and perceptions. Lerner explores how this phenomenon has enslaved us. Surplus powerlessness is defined as a set of feelings and beliefs that make people think of themselves as even more powerless than they are. It leads them to act in ways that actually confirm them in their powerlessness.

With an historical analysis Lerner shows how the phenomenon of surplus powerlessness enslaved the social change movement in the United States. The Left considered how much time and energy were spent to accomplish their goals. Then instead of being encouraged by their successes, the successes were discounted. Victories that could be built on were redefined as failures. Successes in desegregation, and in stopping the Vietnam war, did not translate into further progressive changes. The logical next step would have been to follow up on the War on Poverty. This did not happen. Not only were successes redefined as failures, the Left began to define more and more of the population as "the enemy." There was the assumption that no one would listen. Lerner explains how this illusion of everyone else as an enemy, and thus to be blamed is linked to blaming oneself. Eventually there was a perception that everyone was bad. This led to the perception that if I am bad, then maybe I need to change myself, rather than change society. The effect of all this was a deflection of the social change movement into the individual self-fulfillment movements of the 1970s.[74]

Surplus powerlessness is not just an individual phenomenon. It is most powerful when it manifests itself through our Social Unconscious, that is, the shared meaning that the people in the society assume. What is this shared meaning? It is the model that we all assume is true, the model of how we look at the world. The old model encompasses aspects such as linear cause and effect models of reality and assumes that people are isolated individuals. This is amplified to mean that we have to win at all costs, and that the other person is our enemy. Power means not only the ability to win the fight, but to have control over the other person, and indeed of the whole situation. Any means to achieve this end are acceptable. The model is sacred, and cannot be challenged or changed. It is glorified through "the myth of redemptive violence."[75] Lerner concluded that the whole population feels powerless. It is not only the social activist who feels powerless. The social activists are one specific case. There is a feeling of surplus powerlessness within the whole population.

Are Lerner's conclusions also true for us in Canada? I started to observe others. The more I watched interactions between people, the more I realized how pervasive anger is. Although depression is clearly present, anger seems to lurk just below the surface. More and more I saw the anger emerging. I constantly saw people who not only were angry in specific situations, but they seemed to be stuck in powerless rage.

If more and more people are living their lives in anger,

how do they cope with this anger? I went out and began to ask people what they did with their anger. I asked numerous people who deeply care about their neighbours how they dealt with their anger. For some the response was denial of anger. For others there is the assumption that anger is a natural and automatic response to the world we find ourselves in. It is assumed that it is almost like a force of nature that can be used for good or evil. The people I talked to seem to experience anger as an untamed beast that we have to push down. I was amazed at how many people acknowledge their anger, and who know that they deal with it by deliberately pushing it down and holding it there.

For some the anger is let out in a structured way. One of the people at the Workers Organizing Resource Centre began to talk about his involvement with the Men's Movement. I know little about this movement, but I do know there is a recognition of anger, and that anger has to be dealt with. My friend talked about being given permission to let out all the anger. There is a process of screaming it out, acknowledging the anger is there and allowing yourself to express it. He demonstrated this for me. We had been sitting having lunch in the large common room. He got up from his chair and started to yell. I was amazed at the level of anger that he expressed because I had always experienced him as a kind and gentle person. He had trusted me enough to show me how he dealt with anger. For him and for many other men it is a cathartic exercise. My first response was that I could not see how this would be helpful for me. He said that not all women found this process helpful, but some did.

My friend recommended that I read *Women who Run with the Wolves*. In this book there is discussion of anger as rage. At one point Clarissa Estes says that "the clearing of residual rage must be a periodic hygienic ritual." This seems to be close to the rituals of the Men's Movement. The rage is assumed. It is also assumed that in certain situations it is appropriate. There is an acceptance of "righteous rage." Estes explores how women use rage as a means of empowering themselves. Why does she encourage us to embrace rage? She assumes that getting angry is a way to shift out of the victim role. Those who feel they are powerless victims need to make some kind of major shift in the way they think and feel and live their lives. Estes is not the only writer who encourages people to shift out of the victim stance of fear, despair and guilt/blame into anger. Most of the authors on anger encourage people to welcome and to use their anger, or righteous rage. Many people are led to anger and left there. Estes is one of the few writers who recognize that anger is not a good place to stay, and that another shift is necessary. She recognizes that the rage is not always appropriate. The rage is a fire that burns one's energy. To be stuck in rage means to be "tired all the time, to have a thick level of cynicism and to feel helpless."

At the moment I read this definition of the rage that burns one's energy I knew that I had reached that place. I knew how much I wanted to be healed. For some people the process of healing starts when they make a decision to change. Making the decision itself may not create the changes we want, but it is a way to shift our patterns. It is a beginning. For me the decision that anger was no longer an acceptable way to live my life was the beginning of a long process. My task now was to find and to identify with those people who have found a way to shift their perceptions, and thus their feelings. Thankfully, I knew people in the anti-poverty movement who were not stuck in anger.

One day I had coffee with a good friend. Even though we had worked together in CANE for four years I had never talked to her about anger. She, like myself, had been an activist in the 1960s, and still is today. I asked her how she was able to continue to work on social issues and how she dealt with anger. In her reply she gave me an example. She said that the other day she was reading a letter to the editor from someone in Molson's justifying laying off workers. She said that she could feel herself immediately getting angry, and then she stopped. She said to herself "People will see through this. I do not need to get angry." Then she told me that she had decided a long time ago not to get angry. She realized that things take a long time to change. Therefore she would focus on some area where she could make a difference. She also decided that she wanted to enjoy what she was doing. Her decision meant that she has been able to focus on the work she could do. Today she is an effective advocate for people. I love working with her. Whenever things seem to be going off the track she will smile, and say "That's okay."

In 1999 the Western Canada Poor People's Conference was in Surrey, BC. During the Saturday supper of the conference I sat and talked with Janice. I had known Janice from the days when we were both on the National Anti-Poverty Organization board. I had always been impressed by her quiet wisdom, but had never seriously talked to her about anger. During the meal we shared our journeys. I asked her how she dealt with anger. She talked about assertiveness rather than aggression. She talked about time, and practice to change our responses. As we talked I realized that she was saying things that I knew. I had learned how to move from anger to peaceful strength in my family. The same process holds true within a community.

In families and in communities we need to change our beliefs and perceptions, and one of the most helpful places to look for how to change perceptions is to use reframing techniques. I keep working at this, and keep finding new ways to change perception. For example, we can break the pattern of feeling like a victim by changing the questions we ask. Questions such as "Why me?" are disempowering. On the other hand questions such as "What is great about this problem?" and "How can I enjoy the process while I do what is necessary?" are empowering. Robert and I have a project these days. We are seeking out ways to enjoy life and to have more fun.

Not only can we change our perceptions about our own lives, there are a multitude of ways to change how we perceive other people. Our daughter Catharine was complaining bitterly about some people who had not lived up to her expectations. She was angry they had not fulfilled their responsibilities. Her husband Shane came along and said "Catharine, they are just learning." In our family this is now a standard response if someone is not doing what we think they should. Instead of getting angry we laugh and say "They are just learning."

When we change our way of looking at others, we can begin to really believe that everyone is doing the best they can. At that point forgiveness becomes a possibility.

All "how to" techniques work, but for me they were not enough to make the transformation I longed for. Even though I was able to make a decision to change; even though I was able to change my perceptions and beliefs; even though I was able to forgive; even though I was able to access more and more resources; my anger still lurked within, and could erupt whenever I confronted injustice. It gradually became clear to me that as I struggled to get rid of the anger I had nothing to replace it with. I rejected my anger, and found to my horror that as I reduced my anger I was becoming aware of my emptiness.

The Emptiness of the Shadow Warrior

I now had to face my emptiness and to name it. I could not move from the old paradigm of control to the new one of harmony until I had done this. I had to ask myself "Who am I?" I had always considered myself a justice-seeker and that included being a fighter for justice. Although I had not consciously thought of myself as a warrior, it gradually became clear that was my persona. Carol Pearson in *Awakening the Heroes Within* says that the warrior myth is at the root of all revolutionary struggles of all oppressed people everywhere. Although I recognize that such a statement may be an exaggeration, the warrior myth does seem to turn up everywhere.

There is a vast literature exploring the warrior myth. Most deal with men. However, my daughter recently gave me a book by Antonia Fraser called *The Warrior Queens*. She traces the warrior queen in Britain from Boadicia in AD 60 to Margaret Thatcher. The warrior from the past who I have always identified with was Joan of Arc. Sharing the name must surely be a great influence. Even though my mother never thought of such a thing, I remember as a child telling my friends that I was named after Joan of Arc. Later, when I had read *St. Joan* and saw *The Lark* performed, I identified with the incredible struggle to be true to oneself regardless of the consequences.

There is another side to the warrior myth. We seldom think about how the English saw Joan. To them she was a witch to be burned. Depending on the side you are on, the warrior may represent the forces of good or evil. Depending on who you are, and the gods you serve, the warrior may be good or evil incarnate. The Warrior is an archetype in Jungian analysis, and each archetype has two contrasting identities. Each person may either be unbalanced, or living in harmony. The idea of two opposing parts of the same force is unconscious and mythic. People like George Lucas are so successful because they tap into the mythic images. Everyone recognizes the power of "the force." And we know the dark side of the force exists. Darth Vader thinks nothing of destroying whole worlds. The warriors of today think nothing of destroying our world, our eco-system. We live in the time of the Shadow Warrior.

The shadow warriors in Canada are often in business suits. Their goal is winning at any cost. In the private sector the warrior engages in hostile take-overs. In the public sector the warriors engage in a war of words. The commentators look for the knock-out punch. The warrior is the soldier who defeats the enemy, whose goal is control and power over the other. The enemy is dehumanized and objectified.

All who write about the shadow warrior speak of our desperate need to control others, and our resulting feelings of powerlessness and emptiness. Emptiness is the end result of the need to control. People fear they will lose their identity if they give up their anger and hate. Those who rely on anger create an enemy in order to know they really exist.[76] Those who believe they are winning their war have a smiling mask of control. Those who believe they are losing often show the rage of powerlessness. In the end all are empty.

Discovering the Bright Warrior

We were now fully into the election race. Elections are one of the few times when the general public comes out to listen to, and to question the politicians. Every group tries to get them to come and to speak. The candidates pick and choose where they will go. Once a Minister decides to attend a meeting all the other parties send their "big guns." There had to be a meeting somewhere on poverty issues. The Social Planning Council was able to put one together. So a town hall meeting was set up at Broadway Disciples church, the church across from the Legislature. The large room was packed. I knew many of the people there. Everyone interested in poverty issues had come out because Bonnie Mitchelson, the Minister of Social Services was on the panel. On the stage were the representatives of the six parties running in the Manitoba election. There was Mitchelson from the Conservatives and someone from the Liberals, and the NDP. The three smaller parties Libertarian, Communist and Green were also there. I listened to them all. Although I heard a lot of nonsense from some of the speakers, I did not feel angry. I was monitoring myself, checking my responses. I felt that I was getting a handle on my emotional responses.

Then a person I had heard before at other conferences got up to ask a question. Without a thought my anger rose. I wanted to yell at him, this really bad person. Why? I could handle the rest. As I look back I realize that he was representing himself as a Christian. How could this person call himself a follower of the teachings of Jesus, who loves us, forgives us and calls us to love and serve others? This man seeks to punish and control the "bad people." I believe that he has twisted a message of love into a message of hate. To my amazement I realize that I want to protect Jesus and his message. How ridiculous that seems now. I realized that I saw myself as protector. This was one of the turning points for me in my struggle to understand who I am.

At this point I had two options. Either I could identify myself as "protector," or I could reclaim the term "warrior." Others have changed the term. For example, Jane Jacobs uses the term Guardian.[77] The other choice is to add a qualifying term such as peaceful warrior, awakened warrior, eco-warrior, etc. Even when we add a qualifier there is some uneasiness with the term. Walter Wink asks if the ancient archetype of the warrior can be transformed into a spiritual warrior. He worries that the warrior image will feed the myth of redemptive violence. He questions whether it is possible to claim the warrior virtues without being swallowed by the shadow warrior and the cult of domination. These are important considerations that need to be struggled with.

Writers are cautious about the term warrior because most people today have forgotten what the positive warrior virtues are. The warrior role models that we have tend to be negative. For example, in Winnipeg there is a notorious drug gang called the Manitoba Warriors. Even so, I believe that it is possible to rediscover the attributes, virtues and strategies of the warrior. The task is a lifelong one of mastery, and it is one I am just beginning. Because our culture glorifies the Shadow Warrior, I have decided that it is probably necessary to use a qualifying adjective. If my goal is to achieve peaceful strength, then my identity will be the Bright Warrior.

1) Warrior's Vision

A vision gradually becomes clearer as people and groups discover that they have a common goal. It is true that different groups have different agendas, but we can find those places where we share a common goal. An article in the Globe and Mail showed that even people who seem totally different, with seemingly little in common can find common goals and work together.[78] The headline read "Jews, Natives connect to help Toronto's homeless." People from two very different groups happened to meet when their booths were placed side by side at one of the human rights celebrations. Ms. Capreol, from the native group Na-Me-Res, and Mr. Rosenweing from Ve'ahavta (and you shall love) eventually joined forces to provide food and clothing for the homeless in Toronto. For the Jewish community there was a process of consciousness raising, and for the native community there was a new and unexpected source of needed resources.

More and more people and groups are seeking to work

together as they challenge current systems. At the meeting of the World Trade Organization in Seattle in the fall of 1999 a multitude of groups from all over the world showed up. There were environmentalists, unions, poverty and justice groups, all aware that the direction the WTO was taking would be destructive to us all.

It is not enough just to say what is wrong. We desperately need the discipline required to create an alternative vision. There are many people struggling to articulate a vision of harmony, interdependence and community.

People enmeshed in bureaucratic addictive organizations are struggling to find new ways to bring about reconciliation. For example, the struggle to create alternative and restorative justice systems has gained momentum. Our Aboriginal brothers and sisters in Australia have developed an alternative justice system that is now used for all young offenders. Even here in Winnipeg there is a small group of people creating healing circles for young offenders. All of our formal systems such as justice, education and health are struggling to find new ways. Many people also seek new ways for the informal systems of family and community to live together in harmony.

Ironically, the system that is most destructive is our economic system. Although many people are struggling to articulate an alternative economic system, there is practically no debate within the media or any of the political parties. The public debate is still between capitalism and communism. Those who are thinking and writing about Green Economics speak about the failure of both capitalism and communism.[79] Both are part of the old paradigm. New paradigm thinking changes our way of understanding everything from linear cause and effect to system theory. I was beginning to think that new paradigm thinking was impossible in the realm of economics, but Jane Jacobs new book *The Nature of Economics* blends together nature and economics using system theory.

There is more and more thinking about how to encompass both economics and the environment. The inter-denominational church group called Ten Days for Global Justice has a three year program based on the theme of Jubilee. Two subjects of interest, economics and environment, are part of the discussion. The challenge is to integrate all areas of our lives, to balance the individual and the group, and to include both body and spirit.

The women's movement recognizes the need for balance between body and spirit when they sing about both "bread and roses." The challenge is to take seriously a vision of the interdependent global community where each person is valued and included. This vision of an interdependent world is still evolving. The common threads through all the systems and within all groups of people are beginning to be woven into a tapestry.

In the past when people came together to find common ground, and a common vision, they would create a Charter or Manifesto, in order to share their vision with the broader community. In Canada there was a group of Christian thinkers who created the Fellowship for a Christian Social Order. They set out the identity of this Christian Socialist organization through resolutions. When the CCF, the predecessor of the NDP, was founded in 1932 many of these people were involved with articulating the vision of the party. They, with farm and labour groups and other intellectuals, came together to create the Regina Manifesto.

In South Africa in June, 1955 the African National Congress held a Congress of the People and issued a Freedom Charter. Its aims were for a non-racial democratic South Africa where wealth and land was shared. Human rights, work, education, health, housing and culture would be available to everyone. Nothing in the history of the liberation movement in South Africa caught the popular imagination as this did.[80]

I am continually struggling to find and express an alternative vision. One day I was thinking about the Marxist principle "from each according to their abilities; to each according to their needs." This idea seemed to be based on a contractual relationship between people. My vision needs to express how each one of us lives in relationship and in community. So I took an old idea and shifted it into a new paradigm. I now say:

"From each the gift they have to offer;
To each their place in the circle."

2) Warrior's Way – Discipline

One of the articles on the demonstrations in Seattle against the World Trade Organization quoted Tom d'Aquino, head of the Business Council on National Issues (BCNI), that bastion of corporate Canada. To my amazement he actually said that those leaders of globalization and world wide, unfettered capitalism were like the Spartans holding the pass at Thermopylae. This immediately caught my attention because I had just finished reading *Gates of Fire*, a fictionalized account of the Spartans at Thermopylae. It was a book that normally I would have passed by, but I had been struggling to understand who a warrior is, and what a warrior does.

The vision of the Spartan warrior must be deep in the consciousness of our culture if both Tom d'Aquino and I refer to those warriors. Unfortunately, d'Aquino could not have more than a passing acquaintance with what that battle, and those warriors were about. The key to the Spartan warriors was the creation of a disciplined self within a disciplined community. The goal was to protect and, when necessary, to sacrifice everything for the community.

Over and over again in my search for the warrior I encountered exploration of these characteristics. One cannot be a warrior without discipline. The discipline is the four fold discipline of mind, body, spirit and emotions. Each aspect is equally important. The idea of living a disciplined life excites me. It is so contrary to the consumer lifestyle the envelops and smothers us.

Part of me had always recognized the importance of focusing on how I live my life. I have a quote in my office by belle hooks that says "Staying well is a radical form of resistance." In the past I recognized the wisdom of this advice, but I had never taken it seriously. The discipline was seen as a duty, a dreary duty, not a joyful healing process. I had tried to eat properly, to walk and to do yoga, and to take care of myself, but I had never seen this as essential. Now I see the discipline as part of who I am. I have added the spiritual discipline of centering prayer, a form of meditation. I have found people to teach me, and I go to the sessions joyfully. The centering prayer group is part of a community, one of many small communities that are in the state of being created. The work of creating community is also a discipline. If discipline is only for our own individual growth there is no community.

The Spartan discipline was clearly not an individual discipline. The focus was on a joint discipline for the sake of the community. They and other great warriors such as the ancient Romans fought as a group. It took five years to train a legionnaire to fight in total group discipline. It took a lifetime of total commitment to create a Spartan warrior. In both cases shield was linked to shield to protect the total group. In *Gates of Fire* the young hero in a moment of inattention lays down his shield just out of reach. The trainer walks over and breaks his nose. The shield is there for the protection of the whole group and is never to be out of reach.

The protection of each other is a part of the broader purpose of the warrior. Protection of the whole group to the point of sacrifice was expected. That is what the battle at Thermopylae was all about. The three hundred Spartans held the pass against the Persian king, Xerxes, "the King with half the east at heel," long enough for the Greek city states to meet and develop a common strategy. The Spartans were willing to die, and indeed had spent their lives training for just such a battle. The discipline was by the group for the group. The hope for the future is that we understand that now the group includes everyone and the whole earth.

3) Warrior's Work –Non-Violence

In this century we have seen powerful examples of the Bright Warrior, the warrior who is actively non-violent out of a spiritual discipline. The vision and the action are not separate, but evolve together. Martin Luther King Jr. did not begin the civil rights movement, but responded to the events around him. He gradually took over leadership and gradually came to see a broader and deeper vision than nonsegregated buses.

In the end he had a dream that "all God's children, white and black, would live together in freedom." He saw that this could be accomplished through non-violent means. His article "Pilgrimage to Non-Violence" explores the strategy and the underlying principles. The person using non-violence is passive physically, but active spiritually. The end result is to be redemption and reconciliation. The attack is against the forces of evil, not against people, and the participant is willing to suffer and die rather than physically fight back.

King found both the teachings of Jesus in the Sermon on the Mount and Gandhi's philosophy of satyagraha (soul force) as the basis for non-violent action. Non-violence as a work of power began in South Africa in 1906. On August 22, 1906 the Transvaal government put into legislation an act requiring all Indians above the age of eight to submit to official registration and finger printing. The consequence of refusal would be fines, imprisonment or deportation. On September 11, 1906 Gandhi began non-violent resistance. Eventually he returned to India where he taught satyagraha as a discipline, and used non-violence as the action to bring about change.

In our own country the non-violent struggle for justice is a wonderful legacy that we need to remember, and to build on. I was one of the thousands of people who marched in Winnipeg to force the Conservative government to bring Medicare to Manitoba. In recent years thousands of people have marched in Ontario to protest Conservative government cutbacks on all our social programs. People in Seattle from all over the world have marched against the World Trade Organization, and gone to jail. Today there is a recognition of and acceptance of the strategy of non-violence. What we need to focus on is the vision, the discipline and the heart of the Bright Warrior.

4) The Warrior's Heart: Compassion, Forgiveness, Courage

Here is the core, the place where the energy comes from. What has happened to the heart of the Shadow Warrior? We know what happens to the physical heart of the person who is angry. People who exhibit Type A behaviour, which includes hostility and anger are at risk for a heart attack. What does our spiritual heart risk with anger? It came to me that I was developing a heart of stone. I remembered the prayer of Ezekiel, the Prophet, who prayed that God should turn his heart of stone to a heart of flesh. I shared this passage with the people at CANE one Tuesday. I told them how I had been thinking about my anger, and that I did not want to live like this any more. To my amazement this deeply touched the people at the meeting. It should not have surprised me, for we all yearn for a heart of flesh, loving care for others and for ourselves.

Later I came across a reference to Narnia, that most wonderful fairy tale of C.S. Lewis. Lewis is one of our most popular theologians. His insights are not all in books of theology, but available to us is the fairy stories of Narnia. Aslan, the great lion, comes to Narnia, where it is always winter and never Christmas. He comes to the White Witch's castle and breaths on all the creatures who have been turned to stone. The creatures become alive again. Not only that, there is first a gradual and then a torrent of ice melting and Spring comes again. Aslan does more than bring spring to the land and life to the statues. He touches Edmund, and Edmund's hard and frozen heart is thawed and filled with love.

King has said that "at the centre of non-violence stands the principle of love." We now discover that the warrior is the protector because the warrior loves. The warrior is filled with compassion. The warrior is able to forgive. In 1914 Gandhi negotiated with General Smuts, even though Smuts had broken promises in 1908. When questioned about this Gandhi quoted a Sanskrit proverb. "Forgiveness is the ornament of the brave." The most powerful example we have of both leadership and people who are able to forgive, is in South Africa.[81]

Nelson Mandela and Bishop Tutu's position of forgiveness made it possible for the peaceful transition of power in South Africa. DeKlerk was able to open the door of Nelson Mandela's cell because he knew that there would be no anger or bitter response, and there would be no violent reaction from the people.

Whether one is the leader of a country, or the leader in one's family or community, the transformation from anger to forgiveness can happen in a moment or a lifetime. Unless we recognize the significance of the shift we will live with a hard and angry heart. Forgiveness is the key to escape from rage.[82] Forgiveness does not mean to pretend that the pain did not happen. It involves letting go and it involves a conscious decision to cease to harbour resentment. Every time I see or hear about someone who has made this transformation I am reaffirmed in my belief that it is only love, forgiveness, compassion, harmony that is the hope of the world.

Bright Warriors are often found in communities of people who have suffered. Recently at the Western Canada Poor People's Conference I listened to two native leaders. They did not call themselves leaders. They spoke of themselves as learning from the elders and seeking new visions. The thing that struck me immediately was that there was no anger. Although one man had gone through the residential school system, and had been involved in addictions, he now spoke of healing of all peoples. He led us all in a smudge ceremony with sage on Sunday morning at the conference. Both of the aboriginal leaders sought reconciliation. Neither was bitter. If they chose not to hold anger, who was I to do so?

Bright Warriors are sometimes created by suffering. When I talked to people in Winnipeg about restorative justice I encountered the name of Wilma Derksen. I had heard of the Derksen family a number of years ago. Their daughter Candice had been kidnapped and killed in Winnipeg. This story did not end in feelings of rage and seeking revenge. Wilma Derksen is now actively involved in the restorative justice community. The purpose of this alternative justice is to choose love and compassion to all involved in tragedy. The purpose is to reach out to those who were "the enemy" and to bring them back into the community, to bring them back into the circle.

The heart is finally the place of courage. I learned this lesson many years ago in Winnipeg. Although the details are blurry, the impression is still one of the strongest in my life. I was a teenager, still in high school. I was just beginning to understand how much suffering there was in the world. The suffering did not touch me personally as I was a child of working class parents in the 1950s. But I was gradually recognizing that injustice and suffering were all around me. I also deeply felt the call of Jesus to respond. How did one "feed the sick, cloth the hungry, visit those in prison...?" [83] I knew nothing about politics, about political answers to my questions. I do not remember how I ended up at the old Winnipeg Auditorium one evening, but for the first time I encountered a Bright Warrior. He spoke to my heart, and my heart responded. His vision was clear. There was no violence within him. He called us to stand side by side with him, to work together. And Tommy Douglas said, "Courage my friends. It is not too late to build a better world."

Bright warriors let us go forward singing. I feel like singing and dancing. A great weight has been lifted. The weight of anger. I did not realize how heavy that weight was until it was lifted. Martin Luther King Jr. told us that hate was too great a burden to bear. Although I knew in my mind that he was right, I never understood in my heart. It was not possible for me to understand until I discovered the Bright Warrior. A shift cannot take place until there is a new place to move to. I had to struggle long and hard to find that place. The struggle was shared with Robert, and the ideas were bits of gold found within a vast literature. I do not pretend that the journey is at an end.

I know that it has only begun. My search now is to find other people to share this journey. Already some have gladly said "Can I come too?" I now can truly say that I have found joy, and that joy is peace dancing.

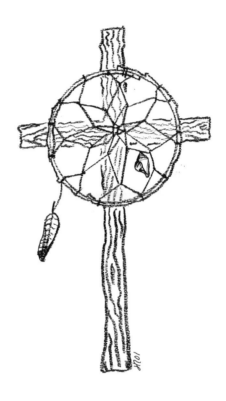

EPILOGUE:
THE WARRIOR'S TALE

T
HERE WAS VERY LITTLE LIGHT. It was not evident whether this was a very cloudy day, or a night of clouds and wind and no stars. The warrior looked up at the sky. Night and day were all the same now, but he remembered sun and moon and stars, and occasionally he would look up.

The ropes that held him were tight, but no longer painful. He was used to them. He didn't struggle. He knew that some food would be provided before he fainted from hunger. It wouldn't be very good or tasty, but it would keep him alive for another day and another night.

Most of the time he sat quietly in front of the big screen. He was thankful that the captors had left the big screen on for him. Another world would appear before him. People laughed and danced and ate and had sex. Sometimes this would change, and people killed, raped and tortured. But that was okay. He knew that soon the beautiful people would come back. There would be more laughing, eating, drinking and sex.

The warrior didn't feel content or happy, but he felt that his life was all that could be expected. After all, he was alive. And that is how he would have spent the rest of his days, but something happened. A memory floated softly into his mind. It came and went with barely a sound. "What was that?" he thought. "I must have imagined it." And he turned up the sound on the big screen, thankful that his hands were able to push the buttons.

Nothing seemed to have changed. Days and nights

passed. Then, to his amazement, he happened to look up, and he saw a star. And he felt something inside. It was joy and pain intertwined, and he began to sob. The tears ran down his face, and he did not know why. A small bright light had entered his heart. So small, but brilliant and shiny. He knew that a wonderful opportunity was before him. He also knew that he did not have to hold on to the starry light. He could allow the light to leave him. He could decide what to do. But the warrior only considered the ropes and the grey sky and the big screen. He could not believe that any other world was possible for him. So the warrior decided to ignore the light, and to focus on the screen. And soon, very soon, the light began to fade. The warrior did not even notice when it left. The action of the big screen was very exciting today or tonight.

What the warrior did not know was that he was not alone. Just out of sight were thousands and thousands of others. All were bound like he was. And each one had seen the star. And each one had a precious memory that softly, softly came. And each one decided whether to open their mind and to let the memory stay. And each one decided whether to welcome the star.

It was very sad that only a very few turned down the sound of the big screen. And even fewer made the amazing decision to turn off the big screen. Most did not even see the off button. But it did happen. Over many years a small number of screens had been turned off. The result was that in a few places the sky was beginning to lighten. Most did not notice this.

Now, at the same time that the sky was beginning to lighten - occasionally- and in a few places, thunderclouds were beginning to gather. There was a rumbling noise that was getting louder. A few drops of rain fell. Now the warrior was outside with no protection except his old ragged cloak. When the first drops fell he pulled the cloak over his head and hardly got wet at all. He thought that nothing had changed for days or years or centuries before. Why was it starting to rain now? This bothered him at first. But he thought that a few drops would not hurt, and he turned up the volume again.

This time when he turned the volume up something strange happened. The people were talking and laughing, but he no longer understood what they were saying. What is happening? Just as he was beginning to panic the words started to make sense again. He knew something unusual had happened. Did the people and the stories and the words on the big screen really make sense? He could not stop thinking about this question. He tried, but the questions never totally went away. He knew that the only way that he could find the answer was to turn off the big screen, but he had not made a decision for so long that he was not sure if he could any more. He looked down and he saw his old ragged cloak. He looked, and he saw the shining pin on the cloak. The pin was shaped like a drum, and in the centre was a cross. The warrior's pin. He pushed the off button.

The warrior just sat there for a long time thinking about nothing, but feeling peaceful. After a while he noticed the tin with a few scraps of food and he realized that he was hungry. He ate it all, even though the fruit was soft and mushy, and the bread was stale. He had eaten worse. He knew that on long journeys, and with hard battles, rations were often short.

How did he know that? He suddenly realized that the memory had come back. A long hard battle had been fought. He had been a captain. There had been thousands of captains and foot soldiers, leaders and supporters. There had been casualties, friends lost, but in the end victory and celebration. The images became clearer and clearer. He had been part of a great battle! How had he come to be here, bound with ropes, with no history and no hope?

The warrior looked around. When there was no light coming from the big screen he could see farther, and things became clearer to him. He began by looking at himself. No-o-o-o!

Surely this was not true. The cloak with the pin covered a shadow. He was alive and ate and could see and hear, but he was a shadow, with no substance. There were no bones, muscle, skin, flesh, blood. All he could really see was a heart, and the heart was stone cold. "I might as well lay down and die" he thought. "There is nothing left of me" At this moment of greatest despair he looked up. And he saw the star.

Some time later he woke up. He looked around at the cold, barren landscape and at the grey sky. He looked at the silent beg screen. He looked at himself. And he saw his heart slowly beating. It was beginning to pump blood through his body, and he was beginning to feel something within him stirring to life. It had been so long since he had considered the possibility of leaving this place of darkness. But now something was happening. It was time to take action. He was a warrior still, even though only a shadow warrior.

The first thing he had to do was to untie the ropes. There must be a way. He looked at the ropes and realized two amazing things. First, there were four ropes all interconnected, and each rope was a different colour. Second, each rope was labeled. At first he could not make out what the letters were spelling. Gradually the letters became clearer. One rope was yellow and the letters spelled Fear. One rope was red and the letters spelled Blame. One rope was blue and the letters spelt Despair. One rope was black and the letters spelt Anger.

Where should he begin? The ropes were different sizes. The black rope was the thickest. It seemed to be covered with black tar. The tar covered the knots, so it was impossible to see how to untie it. One of the other ropes might be easier. There did not seem to be any logical place to begin. Then he began to hear a faint melody. The melody reminded him of an old nursery rhyme.

> *"Begin at the beginning*
> *One step at a time.*
> *God will be with you.*
> *He says' You are mine'"*

The warrior began to hum the old tune, and his heart felt lighter. He began to remember more and more of the old words.

> *"Fear not, I am with you.*
> *You are my warrior still.*
> *Your heart is full of courage.*
> *You have both strength and will."*

As the warrior sang he noticed the yellow rope, the rope of fear, starting to move. Then the warrior remembered that he used to sing this song with his old companions around the campfire. He had been alone for so long that he had assumed all the others had died, or worse had forgotten him, or worse still, had forgotten the cause, the vision, that had brought them together. "No!" he said to himself. "I will free myself, and I will find the others. They must still know the old songs, and I will remind them." And he looked down and the yellow rope was lying on the ground.

Just then there was another sound. Was it thunder? The sound became louder and louder. It was booming and screeching. The sound was like fingernails on slate. The sound was like the crack of a whip. The sound was like wailing, a wailing that went on and on. The red rope began to burn. Gradually, the warrior could make out words within the noise. The words were words of accusation, words of blame and condemnation. The words were ones that he had spoken about others. And the words were ones the others had spoken to him. Words were wounding him. His words were wounding others. The red rope was burning. The heat was becoming unbearable. His eyes filled with tears, as he heard his words adding to the noise. He cried out "Stop!" He cried out "The hate is too much for me to bear!" He cried out "I forgive." And he looked down, and the red rope was lying on the ground.

The warrior fell into a deep sleep. When he woke up the big screen was on. How did that happen? He tried to turn it off, but the Off button did not work. He could move around a bit now that two of the ropes were untied, and on the ground. He inched up to the big screen, and felt all around. Maybe there was another button somewhere. But he could not find anything to push or turn. "There must be someone somewhere else that has control," he thought. "If that is the case then there is nothing I can do." So the warrior decided to sit and watch the big screen. He hoped that eventually the big screen would go silent again, but for now he could do nothing.

So, his old habits came back to him. His days and nights were taken up with eating and sleeping and watching the big screen. And he believed that there was nothing he could do. He did not notice that the blue rope was gradually getting longer and longer. The blue rope was gradually winding around the parts of him where the red and yellow rope had been.

One day the warrior woke up and saw what had happened. The big screen was on. The blue and black ropes covered him. Was the star and the song gone from him? Just then a small soft feather floated down. It landed in his hand. It was pure white, and he gazed at it in wonder. He looked up and saw the tiny white bird flying in circles overhead, and he heard its song. Just when he believed that his song was gone from him he heard the bird's song singing to his heart. He thought "I can sing my song, and the bird can sing my song for me. The ropes can hold me here and the big screen can play, but I can sing my song. No one can stop me." And he began to sing with joy. And he looked down and the blue rope was lying on the ground.

The warrior was filled with thankfulness. The ropes were falling off one by one. Not only that. He realized that his strength was returning. He had not seen it before. The ropes had been around him, but they also had been within him. Somehow their presence had been so powerful that there had been no room for the warrior's power, his physical, mental and spiritual power. But as the ropes left the bone and muscle, the thoughts and feelings, the love and gratitude, hope and faith were growing.

Only the black rope was left. The black rope was still the heaviest, thickest and seemed the most impossible to untie. But the black rope also seemed to be changing. The heavy black rope began to grow longer and longer. One end was untied from the other, and it was changing and changing. Suddenly, the warrior realized that the end had changed into a sword, and the sword was in his hand. The rest of the rope was around the warrior's chest and arms, but his legs were free. He was free to go, and he had a sword in his hand. There was a moment of indecision. Should he seek to untie the black rope, or should he set out holding on to the black sword? He could feel the power of the black sword. He needed power, and after all he had the sword in his hand and thus he controlled it. The warrior stood up, looked around and started out towards where the sky was lightest.

As he walked he heard the rumbling of the thunder. He felt drops of rain. He saw lightening flash across the sky. To his horror the ground itself began to shake. He felt the power of the earth and sea and sky. And he felt the pain. The earth itself was in turmoil and agony. What could he do but continue his search for the others. There must be some of the wise women still left. Surely the elders and the warriors together would know what to do.

After many long hours the warrior climbed a hill. He hoped that he could see some sign to guide him. As he stood on the top of the hill he saw in the distance a figure. He too was seen. They paced towards each other. As they drew closer he saw that the other warrior was also bound with black ropes and carried a black sword. The features of his face were blurred and indistinct.

They met on the plain, and saluted each other. They spoke. The thunder roared overhead. The words were lost in the thunder. They spoke again and again and each time the thunder came. Then more black warriors appeared. Each one held a black sword. Soon the fighting began. Each one fought for survival. Each one fought with hate and bitterness. In the end only the warrior was left alive. His wounds were deep, and he felt the terrible pain, but he was alive. The others were dead, or had left the battle. He could see many on the horizon still holding their black swords. He went to look at the dead. Each time he saw only shadows. Some still wore their cloaks and some still had their warrior's pin. He saw one warrior by a tree who still seemed alive. He came up to the tree, and looked and saw and cried "My brother" and the warrior by the tree closed his eyes and died.

The warrior felt his power going. His wounds were terrible. He was also going to die, to die beside his brother, to die with the black sword in his hand, to die as a shadow, and there would be nothing left. At last he understood. The black rope of hate, anger, rage, bitterness, the black rope had in the end destroyed him. The black sword had only the power to kill, not the power to heal. He dropped the black sword from his hand. He knelt by his brother. He knelt on the barren earth and sobbed.

For a long time he lay with the dead, and wished that he could die. Gradually he became aware of something wet dripping on his hands and on his face. Where the moisture touched him his wounds were beginning to heal. Slowly he raised his eyes and saw that the drips were coming from the tree. It was a healing tree. He knew it now. The old stories had spoken of the healing trees. He had thought the stories were legends from the past, stories for children. But the tree continued to slowly drip a soothing honey coloured liquid. A drop fell near his mouth. He tasted it with his tongue. It tasted of sweet fruit and salt tears. It tasted of healing, sweet as clear spring water, strong as healing spices. He felt his strength returning.

When next the warrior woke he was alone. All that was left was a flock of black crows. They wheeled in the sky, cawing hoarsely. Then they flew off in all directions. Each one was alone crying. The warrior felt like crying too. He felt alone. He felt powerless and afraid. Suddenly, he realized that the tufts of grass that were here and there on the ground were beginning to grow longer and to turn yellow. They were beginning to intertwine together. The warrior looked in amazement. Then he threw back his head and laughed. He laughed with joy. Now he truly understood. The ropes were of his own making. The warrior sang his song.

Begin at the beginning
One step at a time
God will be with you
He says "You are mine"

Fear not, I am with you
You are my warrior still
Your heart is full of courage
You have both strength and will
Brother and sisters
Together we will be
Forgive and love and carry on
All in my company

The warrior walked and sang. He walked in faith until he came to the edge of a forest. He found cool running water, fruits and berries to eat. He made a spear and caught fish in the stream. Here he stayed while his strength returned.

He gradually remembered the warrior's discipline. Every day he exercised and his body grew stronger. Every day he remembered more and more of the old songs, and he composed new songs and his wisdom grew. Every day he made a fire, drew a circle around it and made a cross with stones. He prayed purely and with his whole heart. Finally, he knew it was time to seek the others. He could do no more by himself. The warrior's discipline had healed his body, mind, spirit and will. But light could only come when the company was once again together. Then the darkness would be defeated.

Here ends the Warrior's Tale. The tale of his journey to seek and to find the other Bright Warriors is a tale full of both joy and sorrow. The darkness was still over the land, but the light increased as the company of the Bright Warriors steadily grew. The tale of the coming together of the Bright Warriors is the Tale of The Gathering. It is a tale that only the Bright Warriors know.

END NOTES

1 Winnipeg Sun, October 10, 1994
2 All names of members of CANE have been changed to protect their privacy.
3 Winnipeg Free Press, March 2, 1996
4 Winnipeg Free Press, April 25, 1995
5 Michael Valpy, Globe and Mail
6 William Thorsell, editor-in-chief, Globe and Mail
7 Maclean's, March 20, 1995
8 Senator Erminie Joy Cohen, *Sounding the Alarm: Poverty in Canada*, February, 1997
9 Christina Maslach, *Burnout: the Cost of Caring*
10 Winnipeg Free Press, July 22, 1995
11 Maclean's, February 5, 1996
12 Canadian Labour Congress, *A Good Program in Bad Times: The Dismantling of Unemployment Insurance*
13 Canadian Mental Health Association, *Unemployment: Its Impact on Body and Soul*
14 Seligman, Martin E.P., *Learned Optimism: How to Change Your Mind & Your Life* (Alfred A. Knopf: New York, 1990)
15 Jamie Swift, *Wheel of Fortune*
16 Jamie Swift, *Wheel of Fortune*, p. 75
17 Bruce O'Hara, *Working Harder isn't Working*
18 Canadian Mental Health Association, *Unemployment: Its Impact on Body and Soul*
19 Pat Capponi, *Dispatches from the Poverty Line*, p. 99
20 C. Hamilton, ed., *Reality Check*, p. 20
21 June Crawford, et al. *Emotion and Gender: Constructing Meaning from Memory*
22 Victoria Sherrow, *Violence and the Media*
23 Willard Gaylin, *The Rage Within: Anger in Modern Life*

24 Winnipeg Free Press, November 22, 1997
25 Winnipeg Free Press, March 25, 1993
26 Globe and Mail, May 8, 1998
27 Winnipeg Free Press, April 25, 1998
28 Globe and Mail, April 15, 1998
29 Carroll Saussy, *The Gift of Anger*
30 Jim Stanford, *Paper Boom*, p. 50
31 Globe and Mail, August 30, 1996
32 Globe and Mail, March 28, 1997
33 CBC TV, March 27, 1997
34 Winnipeg Free Press, April 9, 1997
35 Globe and Mail Editorial, April 7, 1997
36 Jamie Swift, *Wheel of Fortune*
37 Winnipeg Sun, March 27, 1997
38 Armine Yalnizyan, *The Growing Gap: A Report on Growing Inequality Between the Rich and Poor in Canada*, (Centre for Social Justice: Toronto, 1998)
39 Duncan Cameron and Ed Finn, *Ten Deficit Myths*
40 Ed Finn, *Canadian Forum*, December, 1994
41 Murray Dobbin, *Taking on the Right: The New Context of Politics*
42 Murray Dobbin, *The Myth of the Good Corporate Citizen*, p. 182
43 Ibid. p. 180
44 Ibid. p. 208
45 Howard Adams, *A Tortured People: the Politics of Colonization*
46 Maude Barlow and James Winter, *The Big Black Book*, pp. 136-137; Richard Siklos, *Shades of Black*, Chapter Eight (Toronto: Reed Books, 1995)
47 Globe and Mail, February 9, 1997
48 Globe and Mail, August 2, 1997
49 Patrick Burman, *Poverty's Bonds*
50 Marlene Webber, *Food for Thought*, p. 35

51 Winnipeg Free Press, August 1996
52 Globe and Mail, December 1997
53 Winnipeg Free Press, June 23, 1996
54 Allan Buchanan, *Charity, Justice and Moral Progress*
55 Ibid.
56 Patrick Burman, *The Moralistic Giving of Charity*
57 Allan Luks, *The Healing Power of Doing Good*
58 Richard Bandler, *Using Your Brain for a Change*
59 Anne Schaef, *Native Wisdom for White Minds*
60 Manitoba Association of Social Workers' Annual General Meeting, May 1998
61 Rev. Robert Campbell, sermon at Westminster United Church, Winnipeg
62 Nelson Mandela, Inaugural Speech upon becoming Prime Minister of South Africa
63 Bhiksuni Pema Chodron, *Prayers for a Thousand Years*, p. 63
64 Karen Holden, *Prayers for a Thousand Years*, p. 149
65 belle hooks, *Outlaw Culture*
66 Jane Buchan, *Transformation in Canada's Deep South*
67 Susan Berlin, *Many We Live: Exploring Community*
68 Helen Forsey, *Circles of Strength: Community Alternative to Alienation*
69 Jim Wallace, Sojourners Call to Renewal newsletter, Vol. 5, No. 1
70 Bill McKibben, *Hope, Human and Wild*
71 Thomas Merton, *Letter to a Young Activist*, February 21, 1966
72 Michael Czerny and Jamie Swift, *Getting Started on Social Analysis*
73 Globe and Mail, August 5, 1999
74 Another contributing factor is that many activists felt that the battles had been won. Kenneth Galbraith explores this in *The Culture of Contentment*

75 Walter Wink, *The Powers That Be*
76 Sharif Abdullah, *The Power of One - Authentic Leadership in Turbulent Times*
77 Jane Jacobs *Systems of Survival*
78 November 15, 1999
79 Paul Ekins, *The Gaia Atlas of GREEN Economics*, p. 76
80 Brian Frost, *Struggling to Forgive*
81 Ibid.
82 Clarissa Estes, *Women Who Run with the Wolves*
83 Gospel of Matthew, Chapter 25

BIBLIOGRAPHY

Abdullah, Sharif M. *The Power of One: Authentic Leadership in Turbulent Times.*
Toronto: New Society Publishers, 1998.

Adams, Howard. *A Tortured People: The Politics of Colonization.*
Penticton, BC: Theytus Books, 1995.

Barlow, Maude, and Bruce Campbell. *Straight Through the Heart: How the Liberals Abandoned the Just Society.*
Toronto: Harper Collins, 1995.

Barlow, Maude, and James Winter. *The Big Black Book: The Essential Views of Conrad and Barbara Amiel Black.*
Toronto: Stoddart, 1997.

Bashevkin, Sylvia B. *True Patriot Love: The Politics of Canadian Nationalism.* Toronto: Oxford University Press, 1991.

Bellan, Ruben C. *The Unnecessary Evil: An Answer to Canada's High Unemployment.*
Toronto: McClelland & Stewart, 1986.

Cameron, Duncan, and Ed Finn. *Ten Deficit Myths: The Truth about Government Debts and Why They Don't Justify Cutbacks.*
Ottawa: Canadian Centre for Policy Alternatives, 1995.

Capponi, Pat. *Dispatches from the Poverty Line.*
Toronto: Penguin, 1997.

———. *The War at Home.*
Toronto: Viking, 1999.

Cayley, David. *George Grant in Conversation.*
Concord, ON: Anansi, 1995.

Czerny, Michael, and Jamie Swift. *Getting Started on Social Analysis in Canada.*
Toronto: Between the Lines, 1984.

Estes, Clarissa P. *Women who Run with the Wolves.*
New York: Ballantine, 1995.

Ellul, Jacques. *Hope in the Time of Abandonment.*
New York: Seabury Press, 1977.

Desroches, Leonard. *Allow the Water: Anger, Fear, Power, Work, Sexuality, Community and the Spirituality and Practice of Non-violence.*
Toronto: Dunamis, 1996.

Dobbin, Murray. *In Defence of Public Services.*
Ottawa: Canadian Centre for Policy Alternatives, 1995.

——. *The Myth of the Good Corporate Citizen: Democracy Under the Rule of Big Business.*
Toronto: Stoddart, 1998.

——. *The New Right and How Things Got This Bad.*
Ottawa: Council of Canadians, 1995.

Fox, Matthew. *The Reinvention of Work: A New Vision of Livelihood for Our Time.*
San Francisco: Harper, 1994.

Franklin, Ursula. *The Real World of Technology.*
Toronto: Anansi, 1990.

Freire, Paulo. *Pedagogy of Hope.*
New York: Continuum, 1994.

——. *Pedagogy of the Heart.*
New York: Continuum, 1997.

Frost, Brian. *Struggling to Forgive – Nelson Mandela and South Africa's Search for Reconciliation.*
London: HarperCollins, 1998.

Goudzwaard, Bob, and Harry de Lange. *Beyond Poverty and Affluence: Towards a Canadian Economy of Care.*
Toronto: University of Toronto Press, 1995.

Grant, George. "A Critique of the New Left." *Canada and Radical Social Change.* Ed. D. Roussopoulas.
Montreal: Black Rose Books, 1973.

——. *English Speaking Justice.*
Toronto: Anansi, 1974.

——. *Lament for a Nation: The Defeat of Canadian Nationalism.*
Toronto: McClelland & Stewart, 1965.

Griffiths, Franklyn. *Strong and Free: Canada and the New Sovereignty.*
Toronto: Stoddart, 1996.

Hamilton, C., ed. *Reality Cheque: Telling Our Stories of Life on Welfare in Ontario.*
Toronto: Ontario Social Safety Network, 1997.

hooks, belle. *Outlaw Culture.*
New York: Routledge, 1994.

—. *Teaching to Transgress: Education as the Practice of Freedom.*
New York: Routledge, 1994.

Kirsh, Sharon L. *Unemployment: Its Impact on Body and Soul.*
Toronto: Canadian Mental Health Association, 1983.

Lappe, Frances Moore, and Joseph Collins. *World Hunger: 12 Myths.*
New York: Grove Press, 1986.

Laxer, James. *False God: How the Globalization Myth has Impoverished Canada.*
Toronto: Lester Publishing, 1993.

Leacock, Stephen. *The Unsolved Riddle of Social Justice.*
London: J. Lane, 1922.

Lerner, Michael. *Surplus Powerlessness: The Psychodynamics of Everyday Life and the Psychology of Individual and Social Transformation.*
Oakland, CA: Institute for Labor & Mental Health, 1986.

Lerner, Sally, et al. *Basic Income: Economic Security for All Canadians.*
Toronto: Between the Lines, 1999.

MacAdam, Murray, ed. *From Corporate Greed to Common Good - Canadian Churches and Community Economic Development.*
Ottawa: Novalis, 1998.

Macy, Johanna. *Coming Back to Life - Practices to Reconnect Our Lives, Our World.*
Toronto: New Society Publishers, 1998.

McKibben, Bill. *Hope, Human and Wild: True Stories of Living Lightly on the Earth.*
Boston: Little, Brown and Company, 1995.

McQuaig, Linda. *Shooting the Hippo: Death by Deficit and Other Canadian Myths.*
Toronto: Viking, 1995.

—. *The Wealthy Banker's Wife: The Assault on Equality in Canada.*
Toronto: Penguin, 1993.

Menzies, Heather. *Fast Forward and Out of Control: How Technology is Changing your Life.*
Toronto: MacMillan, 1989.

—. *Whose Brave New World? The Information Highway and the New Economy.*
Toronto: Between the Lines, 1996.

Noble, David F. *Progress Without People: New Technology, Unemployment and the Message of Resistance.*
Toronto: Between the Lines, 1995.

Oates, Wayne E. *Confessions of a Workaholic.*
Nashville, TN: Abingdon Press, 1971.

O'Hara, Bruce. *Working Harder Isn't Working.*
Vancouver: New Star Books, 1993.

O'Neill, John. *The Missing Child in Liberal Theory: Towards a Covenant Theory of Family, Community, Welfare & the Civic State.*
Toronto: University of Toronto Press, 1994.

Quigley, Margaret, and Michael Garvey, eds. *The Dorothy Day Book: A Selection from Her Writings and Readings.*
Springfield, Illinois: Templegate Publishers, 1982.

Ross, Rupert. *Returning to the Teachings: Exploring Aboriginal Justice.*
Toronto: Penguin, 1996.

Schaef, Anne W. *Native Wisdom for White Minds*.
New York: Ballantine, 1995.

—. *The Addictive Organization*.
San Francisco: Harper & Row, 1988.

Stanford, Jim. *Paper Boom: Why Real Prosperity Requires a New Approach to Canada's Economy*. Ottawa: Canadian Centre for Policy Alternatives;
Toronto: Lorimer, 1999.

Swanson, Jean. *Poor-bashing: The Politics of Exclusion*.
Toronto: Between the Lines, 2001.

Swift, Jamie. *Wheel of Fortune: Work and Life in the Age of Falling Expectations*.
Toronto: Between the Lines, 1995.

Ten Days for Global Justice. *The World We Want: Education and Action Guide*.
Toronto: Ten Days for Global Justice, 1997.

Vanier, Jean. *Community and Growth: Our Pilgrimage Together*.
Toronto: Griffin Press, 1979.

Webber, Marlene. *Food for Thought: How Our Dollar Democracy Drove 2 Million Canadians into Foodbanks to Collect Private Charity in Place of Public Justice*.
Toronto: Coach House Press, 1992.

Wink, Walter. *The Powers That Be: Theology for a New Millennium*.
New York: Doubleday, 1998.

INDEX

COLOPHON

The typeface used throughout this book was
originally designed by the monumental
stone cutter Eric Gill.

ABCDEFGHIJKLMNOPQRSTUVWXYZ
abcdefghijklmnopqrstuvwxyz
ABCDEFGHIJKLMNOPQRSTUVWXYZ
abcdefghijklmnopqrstuvwxyz

Originally known as Perpetua, it was commissioned by the
Monotype Corporation and is based on the capital letters
of the nearly 2000 year old Trajan Column in Rome.
While the capital letters show their heritage to
the stonecutter's art, the italic clearly
shows the lineage it owes to
the calligraphers art.

Text is 13.5 points on a leading of 15 points